Glow with Ramadan All Year Long!

A Guide to Elevating Your Body-Mind-Soul Health
Before, During & After the Fast

Glow with Ramadan All Year Long!

A Guide to Elevating Your Body-Mind-Soul Health
Before, During & After the Fast

Written by Laila Qadira Yamini

New Moons Rising Press
Lithia Springs, Ga.

New Moons Rising Press
Lithia Springs, Ga.
www.footstepstowellness.net

Note to the reader: This book is intended as an informational guide. The strategies, approaches and techniques described herein are meant to supplement and not to be a substitute for professional healthcare or treatment. They should not be used to treat a serious ailment without prior consultation with a qualified heath care professional.

Cover design – Amber Nadirah Khan-Robinson
Cover layout – Khalil Ali, Kaligraphics

Fasting is prescribed for you as it was prescribed for those before you, in hopes that you will develop inner regardfulness, preservation and discipline.
The Holy Quran 2:183

Foreword

When you sit at the table; "Eat with your right hand." This is an Islamic saying that can be traced to the sayings of Muhammad, The Prophet. This saying has various interpretations, one of which is, "be conscious of what you put in your mouth."

I met Laila Qadira Yamini through MALI's (Muslim American Logic Institute) Qur'anic Arabic learning program. As one of our dedicated students, I found her to be very conscientious about Islam and about healthy living, her professed field of interest. I believe it is her Qur'anic studies combined with her conscientious attitude that has given birth to her writing that relates health and diet with this unique time of the year for Muslims, the fasting month of Ramadan. This is the time of the year that many within the Islamic communities become more aware of not only what they put in their mouth but what they put in their mind; and Laila Qadira makes it clear that the best food for the mind and for the body is the food designed by Allah, The Creator (SWT). This is the food which in its original state guarantees the best wellness plan. Hence, reading the Qu'ran, following the life example of Prophet Muhammad (saw), and consuming whole foods (on all levels) throughout the year becomes the thematic message of Laila Qadira Yamini.

The hoped for result, insha'Allah, is that readers of "Glow with Ramadan All Year Long" will gain a healthy biology that is a prerequisite to a healthy and elevated spirituality. We pray that you enjoy your time in reading this interesting guide.

Salim Mu'min, Founder of M.A.L.I. [Muslim American Logic Institute]

Acknowledgements

All praises are due to Allah (SWT), Highly Glorified and Magnified is He! Never will I cease to be amazed at His Help and Grace which are available when petitioning Him in sincere prayer and when crying out to Him from the deepest part of my soul. Certainly, I did much of both as I labored extra hard to complete this book so as to have it available for readers to begin using before Ramadan. (However, at whatever point you receive this guide during your journey – whether before, during or after Ramadan – insha'Allah, will be the right time for it to benefit you in your quest to reach higher levels of health and wellness.) Thus, I pray that the information in these pages is useful to you, the reader, in a way that is pleasing to Allah.

As always, I want to thank my husband and universal partner, Abdul Jaami Hakim Yamini for his unswerving patience and support in everything I do, but especially in helping me to "birth this baby" as we called it. Also, I want to thank my son and daughters, Tariq, Amber, Hafeeza, and Qiyamah for their loving support and special efforts which helped to make this work possible. Many hearty thanks to my Arabic instructor, Imam Salim Mu'min of M.A.L.I (Muslim American Logic Institute) who consented to write my foreword and for his insightful comments included in the book.

Also, I want to express deep appreciation to health experts (from within our Muslim community) whose contributory comments helped to round out and affirm some of the information presented in these pages: Bertram Brooks, Aqiylah Collins, Malikah Kareem, Aggie Nashid, Haneefah

Salim and Sumayya Allen. And, I deeply appreciate the supportive feedback I received from my dear friend and mentor, Dr. Baiza Muhammad.

In addition, I want to express my love to other family and friends who wrapped their arms (virtual and real) around me giving me many words of encouragement and cheering me on. I also want to thank Chandra Varatharajan, my IIN peer coach, who said when I first uttered the words that I wanted to write this book that she knew I could and I would. And, a special shout out to the talents of my wonderful sister, Electa Abdel-Aziz for her meticulous, eagle-eye editing skills that helped to refine the expression of this message. Last, but not least a gracious thanks to Khalil Ali, who helped me out in a last minute "pinch".

Thank you all. May Allah continue to bless and protect.

A special dedication to Ayah Iman who without her "blessed touch" all may have been lost.

Table of Contents

With Allah's Name, The Merciful Benefactor, The Merciful Redeemer

With every rainbow there's one thereafter. . .
With every Ramadan there's another beyond . . .
Bringing infinite opportunities for hope, growth, strength and renewal.
Moving us closer towards our destiny as khalifah fil'ard.

Introduction – The Intent and Purpose of this Book

Doesn't it seem that the span between Ramadan each year gets a little closer? That as soon as one Ramadan is over the next one is not far behind? Is this perception an illusion related to the speediness of our busy lives or a Sign that the Days of Allah[1] have arrived? Whichever it is, increasingly it is evident that Ramadan is becoming more center stage in our lives. And, that this momentous Month, filled with layer upon layer of blessings, offers us unparalleled opportunities to uniquely shape our development in ways that can last many moons hereafter, if we are proactive in working to sustain its rewards.

Because of the magnitude in purpose and impact of this Blessed Month, it only makes sense that special preparations be made that allow us to best benefit from its multitude of rewards. Foremost, this book is offered as a guide for tweaking your mindset, health habits and daily routine to prepare you for this profound time of the year, which is most favorable for making headway in areas key to your Deen and personal success. A success that not only advances your religious understanding, but also that strengthens your overall intellectual, physical and emotional growth in ways most pleasing to Allah (SWT) and most fulfilling within yourself.

Our Nabi, Prophet Muhammad (saw), the model example of the highest possibilities of human expression when adhering to the Command of Allah in the Holy Qur'an, exemplified sound health on all of these levels. Therefore, in following the footsteps of his Sunnah, it is compulsory for all of us, as believing Muslims, to strive to do the same.

Certainly Ramadan is the optimum time to work towards actualizing every aspect of our human potential. This manual, however, does not give detailed instructions about the obligatory or recommended practices regarding the Fast itself. I am assuming you already know what these are or that you can readily get this information from another source (i.e. an imam, books, articles).

It is my intention, though, for you to view this manual as an accompaniment to every book you've read or lecture you've heard that explains the intricacies of the uniqueness and richness of this special time.

Why? Because this manual is intended as a *useful guide* containing information, exercises and recommended activities that provide a gateway for reaching a higher level of consciousness through which you can experience the full range of Ramadan's blessings designed by Allah for you!

Here is what you can expect from following the practical guidelines contained within these pages:

- Improved energy and vitality throughout your days of fasting
- Greater productivity in making spiritual gains during the Fast
- Increased motivation to engage in supererogatory acts during the Fast
- Inspiration for proactively pursuing goals related to your overall development
- Opportunities for holistic healing – body, mind and soul – that will benefit you far beyond your fasting experience
- And much more . . .

In chapters 1 – 5 you are led through a process for: conditioning and focusing your mindset as you approach Ramadan; assessing the current level of your body, mind and soul health; then creating a personal vision for a more empowered state of being throughout your Fast and beyond.

In chapters 6 – 8 information is presented on the vital factors that most impact your health. Each of these chapters is divided into three parts – what you need to do in that area to *cultivate better habits and practices to prepare for Ramadan,* what you need to do in that area to *maintain* these *habits and practices during Ramadan* and what you need to do in that area to *sustain these habits and practices after Ramadan.*

Chapters 9 - 15 outline additional factors critical to your health, well-being and personal success – spiritually, mentally, emotionally and physically. You will also find recipes and meal preparation tools in the Appendices section. Included as a special bonus is a journal template that you can use to track your thoughts, feelings and progress as you travel on your journey through this beautiful and incredible life-defining month.

Since this manual is meant to be interactive by having you write responses to corresponding exercises and questions in each section, I suggest that you get a special notebook to record your answers and to keep as a record of all the wonderful insights and inspiration you will receive this month, insha'Allah.

Ramadan Mubarak! My prayers are that all of you will have a magnificent fruitful journey as you enter the sanctuary of this Most Blessed Month and that the glow of success you attain during this time (inner and outer) be sustained until you enter the threshold of Ramadan once again next year! Ameen!

Chapter 1 - Cultivating a New Mindset for Ramadan

We have indeed created man in the best of molds.
Al-Quran 95:4

A few weeks or even a couple months before the start of a new Ramadan season many of us are not only eager, but restless for it to begin. Our souls are crying out. We've gone through our struggles and scrapes for the year, sometimes intensifying in Shaban (the month preceding Ramadan), and now we're anxiously anticipating day by day the moment we actually enter the Blessed Month. At that time like no other, we probably feel most like *real* Muslims living and worshipping in *real* Muslim communities. We're striving extra hard to make our five daily prayers on schedule, to read Qur'an *every* day, to do numerous charitable acts and of course to seek the ultimate achievement commanded of us during this month – sacrificing for Allah's Pleasure by abstaining from food, drink (and lawful) sex during daylight hours each and every day for a whole month.

Not only are we realizing greater fulfillment in our Deen by intensifying our personal religious practices, but we are feeling a closer alignment with many of our Muslim brothers and sisters all across the planet engaged in these same rituals with joyful hearts on their best Islamic behavior.

For an entire month there's a wonderful vibration of positivity humming in Muslim communities throughout the world and there's a unity within the ummat quite unlike any other time during the year. Most of all we have an opportunity to come into a special connection and closeness to our Lord that engulfs us with breathtaking humility, piety and obedience to His Command. And we begin developing a glow from within that radiates beauty, peace and serenity – making us feel vibrantly alive – at one with Our Creator and His creation!

Then the Eid festivities and celebration arrives! With it, the joy and exhilaration of accomplishment! For a while we're able to maintain the buoyancy and peace that are the immediate residuals of the Fast. But after a while, the spiritual, mental and physical benefits acquired considerably slack off. We may sustain a few weeks consistency in reading Qur'an, in making prayers on time and eating in smaller amounts, but usually once again our busy, busy lives start getting in the way and we settle into our automatic routines reverting to many of our same habits and personal challenges.

With the same mindset and habits, the same types of stressful and challenging situations previously experienced start cropping up throughout the year. Then, we're back to where we were – until we go into the next Ramadan.

We need to break this cycle of attaining highs during the Fast that lapse into lows a few weeks or months later. This yo-yoing back and forth from year to year stunts our personal growth and invariably the growth and productivity of our communities.

Following this guide will help you optimize your Ramadan so that you enter the next Ramadan on a much higher level than you started the year before – physically, mentally, emotionally and spiritually. As a result, the benefits you receive from the Fast will prove more sustaining in the days, weeks and months beyond its completion. You will become more active, energized and productive than ever; capable of contributing more to your families, your communities and the world around you.

Reflection:
1. What are some of the challenges you've faced leading up to this Ramadan?

2. Which of these challenges have you experienced in previous years?

3. How are you committed to approach your challenges differently starting this Ramadan?

Chapter 2 – A Unique Opportunity in the Blessed Month

Behold thy Lord said to the angels: I will create
a vicegerent (khalifah) on earth . . .
Al-Quran 2:30

What is the purpose of Ramadan? We all know the obvious answer – to fast for the Pleasure of Allah. Surely Allah created mankind for His worship alone. And, one of the highest and most revered forms of worship is in His Command to fast during this Holy Month of the Islamic calendar. No one is exempt unless sick, mentally incompetent or on a journey. Truly Ramadan is an exceptional event in the lives of Muslims; therefore to participate in such a meritorious affair, at a time of unprecedented rewards and blessings, requires that we exert our best efforts.

What is the best way to prepare for this magnanimous occasion? When and how do we begin?

Making preparations at least a few weeks before the new moon for Ramadan is sighted is wise. This means taking time out for reflection, planning and conditioning yourself not only with practice fasts, but through realigning your actions, and even your thoughts, so that you enter Ramadan with a focused momentum, a softened heart and a laser determination. Not only so you can more easily submit to the requisites of the Fast, but so you will be empowered to get the highest benefit from your fasting experience.

Let's reflect for a moment on what it means to Fast for the Pleasure of Allah. What is Allah really saying, or perhaps an easier question to answer is, what is He *not* saying? Truly Allah receives nothing added by His human creatures fasting or doing anything else for His Pleasure. He is One, Eternal and Absolute and He has no need for one iota of anything for His sustenance or fulfillment! So, fasting is for Allah's Pleasure because He unequivocally states that it is, but it can't be for His Benefit. Thus, as His human created servants, it must be for our benefit. And what could possibly be the benefit that Allah intends for us?

He tells us in His Book, the Holy Qur'an, that He created man to be a vicegerent or caretaker on the earth. This is a role of leadership in which an individual, man or woman, is capable of providing care, oversight and stewardship for any and everything Allah has produced on the earth. The khalifah, the word in Arabic for vicegerent, is one who has surrendered his or her will to Allah whereby the forces of nature and the created matter on the earth come fully into their service.

Yet before a person can reach khalifah status and take care of many people and environments on the earth, he or she must develop the consciousness and the ability to take care of their individual self. This necessitates that the body, mind, and soul of the person become sound, intact and in a state of optimal health and well-being. How can anyone who is in ill-health, whether physically, mentally or spiritually, be wholly entrusted with the care of others?

Thus, Ramadan, a time for cleansing, purification and renewal, is a prime opportunity for believers to come into a healthier conditioning of body, mind and soul so their consciousness for attaining the role of khalifah is more finely attuned. The Fast – the abstinence of food and drink during the daylight hours, praying, reading of Qur'an and the charitable acts we are encouraged to perform are actually Divinely designed tools for our personal growth and elevation on all levels. It is during Ramadan that we deepen our consciousness and capacity for reaching the height of our human potential as khalifah fil'ard – the caretakers of the earth!

If you can accept this line of reasoning as a fundamental purpose of Ramadan, then it's simple to see that striving to live into this purpose and attain objectives related to it is when we become most pleasing to Allah. The Fast is not simply to satisfy the requirements for fulfilling the ritualistic practices of Ramadan, but for using this Divinely ordained month, with its special tools and special blessings, as a special time to grow and develop in phenomenal ways. Ways which will allow you to contribute your unique gifts and talents more deeply and expansively to your family, community, humanity and the environment around you.

Ramadan is an opportunity for accelerating light years ahead in our human development, and when it ends to remain capable of sustaining this level of personal success until we enter the next Ramadan where we again travel light years on our journey towards reaching our human completion as khalifah fil'ard. Can you see it – your human body carrying intellect, soul and form evolving over time; like a spacecraft rushing past the stars in the universe coursing its way through the infinite spaces of time? To reach a pre-determined (and wonderfully magnificent) destination for your highest achievement as decreed by the Gracious, Bountiful Creator of us all!

The tips and guidelines in this manual will enhance the journey you've already begun. It is designed to show you how, with much more awareness, to engage your natural human faculties of sight, hearing, feeling and intellect to connect with the natural elements of air, water and food to enhance your use of Ramadan's Divinely decreed tools of abstinence, prayer, Qur'anic reading and charitable acts. Insha'Allah, the heightened synergistic interaction between these dynamics will yield a more enlightened and productive Ramadan than you've ever experienced.

Reflection:
1. Name 3 ways you feel you can improve in order to better take care of others and the environment around you.

2. Before you go to the next section write the current condition of your health – physically, mentally, emotionally and spiritually.

Chapter 3 – Assessing Where You are Now

And Allah has produced you from the earth, growing gradually . . .
Al-Quran 71:17

Before embarking on any journey we have to identify our starting point and the destination where we want to end up. This logic applies not only to physical travel, but also when beginning an inward journey of the soul – as Ramadan certainly is for those who view it as the highest spiritual-advancing venture we are commanded by our Lord to participate in each year.

Though it is our soul that receives the ultimate benefit from Ramadan, we must also strive for healthy improvement in our bodies and intellect as well. Having sound health in all three areas – body, mind and soul – will ensure the level of balance we need in order to achieve the higher levels of productivity and achievement we are seeking to carry us throughout the coming year. In order to determine a starting point for improving your health, holistically, during Ramadan, a brief survey entitled **Your Personal Earth** is at the end of this chapter to help you assess where you currently are.

Just as the earth is composed of approximately 75% water with the remainder land mass, your body is about the same – 75% water with the rest tissue and bone mass. Just as the earth needs quality water, food, air and sunlight to grow and produce, your body needs the same. And just as your body needs tender loving care for it to develop and thrive, you also need large doses of loving relationships to do the same.

If you have doubt as to the impact of these vital factors on the ability of the earth to grow and reproduce (which is its purpose) then look at the plants below to reflect on how "what grows from the earth" can look if it is deprived of any one of them.

Which one are you?

Your purpose is to also grow and produce. Not only so you can reproduce children and generate material goods, but so you are capable of producing ideas, strategies, and actions to move your life forward towards full expression.

As a result, you will not just be surviving from day to day, but living with vitality and the ability to evolve and thrive! In finding your purpose you will find your life is more meaningful and full of contributions, inspiration and support for others – whether within your family, neighborhood, community or any environment where you are actively involved.

However, common wisdom says that it takes having the right skills, attitude, and the right finances to thrive in this challenging modern society. Yet, what also are needed are the right factors that create a state of optimal health – the best possible health for **you**. If you don't feel good – i.e. if you have aches, pains, stiffness, chronic illnesses like diabetes or hypertension or even low energy that makes it difficult to hold up till the end of your day, then it is going to be very challenging to do things which allow you to live life to your fullest capacity. Zoning out in front of the TV for long periods, playing endless rounds of electronic games, spending hours on the internet or talking incessantly on the phone may not only be an unproductive use of your time, but may indicate your lack of physical and mental energy to put high powered ideas and plans into action.

Having sufficient energy is important to all of life. All life forms *are* energy and need additional energy to carry out the purpose Allah has willed for them in this life. The foods you consume, even the water you drink contributes to either raising or lowering the level of energy that's in your body. The more energy you have, the more animated and dynamic you can be in the expression of your life. The less energy you have, the less ability you have to live into the potential you were given at birth to unleash during your lifetime.

Where does this energy come from? Certainly Allah (SWT) is the Creator and Primary Source of all energy that moves through and propels His creation. However, the required amounts of energy we need to carry out the daily functions of our lives come through the food and water we consume. Both have varying levels of energy depending on what type they are, where they come from and what nutritive value they carry to your body, mind and soul.

Generally speaking and as a rule of thumb, whole natural foods that grow from the earth and that are not processed (where something has been added or taken away from them in a factory setting) will provide you with much more energy and nutrition than those which come packaged from a manufacturer. The same is true for water. Pure water that comes from a natural spring in the earth is going to carry an energetic force greater than water which comes from a city reservoir that has had chemicals added to render it "drinkable".

There are other earthly elements that provide you with energy in addition to food and water. The air you breathe, the activities and work that you engage in, and your relationships with your mate, your children, parents, friends, and even those whom you may only know casually, give you energy. In each relationship there are different levels of energy that are exchanged depending on their type and quality. All of these energies impact and affect your quality of life, your ability to produce quality thoughts, ideas and actions, and your ability to nurture and raise children who are capable of doing the same.

Look again at the pictures of the two plants. Ask yourself which one you more closely identify with on a daily basis. Do you usually feel vibrant, energetic and lively as indicated by the appearance of the plant in the first picture or do you feel droopy, fatigued and lifeless as represented by the second plant?

Now ask yourself what types of foods are you *mostly* eating every day. Are you eating whole natural foods purchased from the produce section of the grocery store, i.e. those that *don't* come in packaging – because they need no labels to tell you what they are?

Or are you eating packaged foods that carry labeling which lists a string of ingredients, many whose names you can't pronounce or that are made with excessive sugar and salts that you know aren't good for your body?

Whichever category of foods you more frequently eat will usually determine the amount of energy and vitality being produced in your body and will determine your state of health in varying ways.

Other health factors reflected in the survey below also impact your body's state of well-being. Surely, not drinking enough water or drinking a poor quality of water will take its toll on your health, as will not being productively engaged in work that you love and interacting with people who treat you with love and respect.

Ramadan is a time to assess and put forth efforts to remedy many of your lifestyle deficits and negative habits. It is not a time to focus on health for superficial reasons – just for the sake of looking good so you can have pretty skin or lose weight to fit in your clothes better – it is a time for evaluation and implementation of improved health strategies.

Ultimately, the purpose of focusing and seeking to increase better health during Ramadan is to allow us to be a better instrument for receiving Allah's instructions as His khalifah so we can move forward in the development of our individual, family and community lives. We can also contribute to an enhanced life and vibrancy of humanity on this planet. This is the charge given us by our Creator, Allah (SWT) in the Holy Qur'an and this is the drive and determination we must embody to successfully fulfill what Allah has decreed for us as His servants.

Please take the following brief survey to consider where you are right now in your journey of preparing for and participating in the most eventful and momentous endeavor of your life this year – The Holy, Blessed Month of Ramadan!

YOUR PERSONAL EARTH SURVEY

Circle the answer that **best** describes where you are regarding your health right now. *BE HONEST!*

Do you drink plenty of good, **clean water** every day? (½ your weight in ounces of spring or quality filtered water?)
[1 – Rarely   2 – Sometimes   3 – Almost Always]

Do you practice regular **deep breathing**? (Into your abdominal area so oxygen can be distributed more efficiently to all parts of your body)
[1 – Rarely   2 – Sometimes   3 – Almost Always]

Do you get sufficient **nightly rest and sound sleep**? 7 – 8 hrs. or enough so you are not tired, sleepy or have low energy the next day?
[1 – Rarely   2 – Sometimes   3 – Almost Always]

Do you eat good, **quality, whole foods**? (Plenty of fresh produce – fruits and vegetables; particularly dark, leafy vegetables – not foods processed or heavily laden with sugar or salt?)
[1 – Rarely   2 – Sometimes   3 – Almost Always]

Do you **exercise several times a week** for at least 20 minutes? (Stretching as well as aerobic exercise such as walking, swimming, biking, or jogging – exercise you love and commit to?)
[1 – Rarely   2 – Sometimes   3 – Almost Always]

Do you have good **healthy relationships** with family and friends? (That reflect love, respect, appreciation and forgiveness? A strong, loving and intimate relationship with your mate?)
[1 – Rarely   2 – Sometimes   3 – Almost Always]

Do you **enjoy the work that you do** every day? If employed, your job? A business you're developing or at least finding time to do some work you love doing – a hobby or volunteering to help others?
[1 – Rarely   2 – Sometimes   3 – Almost Always]

Do you regularly engage in healthy, **stimulating activities for re-creation**? (Those that re-create your mind and spirit – books, lectures, positive discussions, gardening, nature walks, meditation, picnicking, playing with children . . . ?)
[1 – Rarely   2 – Sometimes   3 – Almost Always]

Do you have a **strong connection with your Creator**? By striving to have an intimate relationship with Him, knowing with certainty, that He is the only One to resolve your problems and mend your heart? Grateful and appreciate for *everything* He has given you – successes *and* challenges?
[1 – Rarely   – Sometimes   3 – Almost Always]

ASSESSING YOUR HOLISTIC LEVEL OF HEALTH RIGHT NOW

1. In which categories are you most challenged (i.e. have the lowest scores)?

2. What 3 things really stand out for you in these areas that you need to address first?

3. Which categories are you strongest in (i.e. have the highest scores)?

4. Identify ways you can improve in at least one of these areas (i.e. go to the next level)?

5. Identify what you are most committed to start doing right now.

Chapter 4 – Envisioning a More Empowered You

When I have fashioned him in due proportion and breathed into him of My spirit fall you (angels) down in obeisance to him.
Al-Quran 38:72

The revelation of Qur'an, The Final Scripture, began on the night of *Lailatul-Qadr* during the month of Ramadan as the Prophet (saw) sat meditating in the Cave of Hirah on Mount Nur. This fateful event was marked by long bouts he'd previously spent in the Cave pondering and contemplating the challenges of his day as he pleaded in du'a to Allah for guidance and resolutions. His constant supplications were finally realized when the Angel Jibril appeared and squeezed him tightly three times in succession with the instruction to *"Read in the Name of Thy Lord . . ."* Thus began the descent of the Last Revelation which would take place over the next 23 years of the Prophet's life addressing every conceivable situation or challenge that mankind would ever encounter in any circumstance, culture or nation throughout time.

In somewhat the same way, but certainly not with the same purpose, intensity or mission given to the Prophet, you have a similar opportunity available during the Month of Ramadan to receive guidance and insights in answer to your du'as to resolve challenges from within and around you – not only when seeking the Night of Power, but any time during the Blessed Month. Of course, these insights and guidance will not be Revelation because we know only prophets receive Revelation and Prophet Muhammad (saw) was the recipient of *The Last Revelation*, The Holy Quran. But what you can hope to receive during Ramadan is divinely inspired guidance rooted in the Qur'an that will address your particular needs and concerns. Therefore, using the Prophet's (saw) example of seeking Allah's guidance through solitary periods of meditation and prayer in the cave prior to the descent of Revelation, it is wise to prepare yourself for receiving Allah's Divine spirit of inspiration (Ruh) during Ramadan by entering a contemplative mindset beforehand that allows you to connect with increased awareness to the deep yearnings within your own soul.

Before exploring this topic further, let us not forget that a major portion of the Prophet's (saw) spiritual and mental prowess rested on a foundation of robust physical health. At the age of three he was raised by Bedouin Arabs for two years to provide him the benefit of clean air, fresh foods and the pristine beauty of the Meccan desert that nourished his early development – body, mind and soul. Many of the Quraish, who became stalwart Muslims, including his Sahaba (close companions), were brought up in similar circumstances as was the custom in Meccan society for children whose parents could afford to do so.

Throughout his life the Prophet (saw) continued to display many capabilities that demonstrated, at all times, that he was in the best of health on all levels of his development. Not only did he excel as a spiritual leader and master strategist, but he also performed very labor intensive activities such as horseback riding, walking long distances by foot, helping to build masajid, engaging in sports and fighting in the heat of grueling battles.

In addition, the Prophet's (saw) heart was said to have been purified by two angels who came to visit him during his childhood sojourn in the desert. It has been recounted in sirah and hadith that they opened his chest and lifted out his heart to cleanse it with white snow. While this story is probably more allegorical than literal, it reflects the purity and sanctity of the Prophet's (saw) true nature (which earned him the title among his peers as Al-Amin) thus setting the stage for his later reception of The Holy Qur'an. All of the incidents and accounts of the Prophet's (saw) life from birth until death demonstrated that he constantly was in possession of a sound body, sound mind and sound heart – free of physical, mental or spiritual dis-ease.

In contrast, many Muslims today are living in countries around the world with health that is continually compromised by infectious and chronic dis-ease. The root of most dis-eases, whether physical, mental or spiritual, is toxins, stress and digestive disorders which can be traced to nutritional, relationship and lifestyle imbalances. The current surge of obesity, a major contributor to serious health conditions, is increasingly on the rise in industrialized nations as well as in developing countries where indigenous cultures have been influenced by the Western lifestyle.

Until 1980, fewer than 1 in 10 people in industrialized countries like the United States were obese. Today, these rates have doubled or tripled. In almost half of these [modern nations] one out of every two people is overweight or obese. These populations are expected to get even heavier in the near future, and in some [of these] countries two out of three people are projected to be obese within 10 years.[2]

However, even in developing-world countries where the poor still go hungry, the new upper and middle classes suffer from diseases caused by eating too much. More than 1.6 billion adults over the age of 15 worldwide are overweight, according to the World Health Organization's latest data, and at least 400 million adults are obese. Taken together, these numbers account for more than a third of people on Earth. In five years, the agency predicts the number of overweight people worldwide will rise to 2.3 billion[3].

Despite obesity often being associated with the intake of too much food, it is now understood to also be the result of the intake of the wrong types of food – food that simply is not nutritious enough or that contains too many harmful ingredients. This includes processed foods as well as produce that have been grown in depleted soils. What is the connection between these inferior foods and obesity? They represent "empty calories"; foods devoid of vital nutrients that rarely allow people to experience true body nourishment and satisfaction – so they overeat.

However, the intense focus on obesity as the *primary* trigger of disease is somewhat a red herring; meaning that it is misleading to believe that being overweight solely leads to an increased onset of dis-ease.

There are many people who are not overweight that are still beset with chronic illnesses. Because the scale doesn't tip past a number you are uncomfortable with doesn't necessarily indicate you are healthy.

What seems to be the true determinant of health is the body's ability to have ample defenses to ward off systemic toxins. Not only are these body poisons coming from environmental sources, but increasingly from bad nutrition. Therefore, though you may be on the thinner side, you may still have a compromised immune system incapable of fighting toxic overload. If so, you too, are vulnerable to dis-ease. Yet and still, toxins often do become trapped in layers of fatty tissue, which intensifies the possibility for infection or inflammation, thus making obesity a *critical factor* in the development of dis-ease.

Stress is also a major culprit for initiating dis-ease because it leads to a poorly functioning immune system and is a factor in the body retaining too much weight. However, much of the stress in this life is unavoidable. After all, Allah created the shaitan to test and strengthen us in this world so that the life challenges we undergo qualify us to become the crown of creation as khalifah fil 'ard. And, doesn't pressure make diamonds? Certainly it is the struggles and stressors of life that often build human character and shape and fortify faith.

Yet, though there are aspects of stress that are inevitable and at times even beneficial, many health conditions can be greatly improved by learning to create healthier responses to stress.

As a result, you'll be able to approach internal and external difficulties with calm and focused faith rather than reactionary worries or kneejerk responses that trigger a release of harmful stress hormones that wreak havoc in the body. But many people, including Muslims, are succumbing to stress-based as well as nutritionally-based illnesses; therefore a change in diet and lifestyle practices is needed to reverse these alarming trends of ill-health in our communities.

Surely Ramadan is a time to take on new disciplines and habits for creating stronger mindsets and bodies, as well as embracing the simple life principles that the Prophet (saw) taught and lived which make him, without doubt, the living example of God's Word as communicated in the Holy Qur'an.

Meditation and reflection coupled with a nutritious diet and balanced life approach are vital to reaching the right level of health that will lead to higher mental and spiritual heights. Embracing these objectives during Ramadan, along with abstaining from food during daylight hours, will optimize your ability to work towards actualizing your human potential more than any other time during the year. Being determined to take on the challenge to improve your strength, vigor and focus will allow you to make the most of your Fast.

At this moment . . . . . right now, I'd like you to pause your reading and find a quiet space to connect with what's going on inside of you. Don't focus on your aches and pains, but on your longings to be whole, complete and at peace within.

In the word "peace" can be found the true definition of health which is reflected in the Arabic word *salima* (the root of the words *Islam, Muslim, salaam*) that embodies not only the idea of obedience and peace, but also the concept of health related to wholeness.

Salima means to be in sound condition; well, free of defects or imperfections. Its meaning suggests prosperity, good health, wholeness and completeness in every way. Therefore, a Muslim who surrenders to the principles of Islam and to the Will of The Creator, Allah (SWT), will come into a state of peace reflected in their ability to be in sound condition – healthy and well – thereby prosperous in every facet of their lives.

NOW, it's time to very intently listen to your voice from within:

- **Take three deep long breaths** bringing your breath in as deeply as possible. Try to sink your breath right below your navel area which in traditional Chinese practices is known as your *dantien*. Deep breathing will oxygenate your body more fully allowing you to be more clear-headed and will also relax any tension and tightness you feel.
- Very gently **place your hand over your heart** (regarded by some as the seat of the soul) and ask yourself – *"What do I long for? What do I really want to happen with my life?" What do I feel needs to change within in order to be productive and able to perform at my best?*
- **Listen very carefully and closely** as your soul, your heart speaks to you in a way that brings to mind your needs and desires for your life's deepest expression; things you know that in doing, you can become more pleasing to Allah and

39

that can bring much satisfaction and fulfillment to you and others.

- Now **briefly write down what you've received** from this conversation coming from deep within. Everything you write may not appear to make sense, but write it down anyway. At this time your soul may be communicating things that you may not have the awareness to understand.

Also, reflect a while on the magnificence of your physical creation – i.e. your personal body. Be in awe of it – not only its physical appearance, but its amazing functions and abilities to perform and endure.

Did you know ...

- Your body gives off enough heat in 30 minutes to bring half a gallon of water to a boil.
- Every tongue print is unique.
- Every day an adult body produces 300 billion new cells.
- You use 200 muscles to take one step.
- Your nose can remember 50,000 different scents.
- Feet have 500,000 sweat glands and can produce more than a pint of sweat a day.
- During your lifetime, you will produce enough saliva to fill two swimming pools.
- Scientists have counted over 500 different liver functions.
- One human hair can support 3.5 ounces.
- The human brain cell can hold 5 times as much information as the Encyclopedia Britannica.
- Nerve impulses to and from the brain travel as fast as 170 miles/hr.
- Every human spent about half an hour as a single cell.
- There are 45 miles (72 km) of nerves in the skin of a human being.

- The average human heart will beat 2.5 billion times in its lifetime and pump 48 million gallons of blood.
- Each square inch (2.5 cm) of human skin consists of 20 feet (6 m) of blood vessels.
- During a 24-hour period, the average human will breathe 23,040 times.
- Human blood travels 60,000 miles (96,540 km) per day on its journey through the body.
- It takes the interaction of 72 different muscles to produce human speech.

As you can see, the human body is created for performance, flexibility and endurance. Not only for athletes and those endowed with above average physical prowess to experience, but so that just about anyone is capable of benefitting from their body's inherent abilities and acquired skills throughout their lives. Preserving the health of your physical body allows it to retain its original purpose as a carrier, a viable vessel for the precious cargo of your human soul.

Yet most people are very dissatisfied and even hate their physical bodies. Mainly, because they are measuring their flesh appearance with a societal standard based on influences and values (particularly from the media) that are false, misleading and artificial. Women projected as rail thin or men portrayed as overly muscular – or those that supposedly have the ideal hair, eye color or body shape – are harmful models to use for evaluating the beauty and function of the flesh body Allah provided as your gift to exist on this earthly plane.

It really doesn't matter how your physical features look on the outside. What counts are how well your organs are performing inside your body and whether your soul is able to attain levels of spiritual purity. True health is rooted in beauty that originates within a sincere heart and a clean body and that radiates outwards. Perhaps though, you are overweight or underweight or challenged with a health condition that distorts your natural appearance which offers some justification in not liking the form your body has taken. More than likely, however, this is the result of what you've *done* to your body and is not an inherent condition that you can't change. Therefore, in most instances, with Allah's Help, you have the power to transform your body's health and appearance if you are committed to do so. Certainly during this special time of Ramadan, like no other, you have the help of Allah and His angels!

Now, review your soul's message; then continue your reflections:

- **Envision yourself engaged in whatever you're longing to do**. *How does your body feel? What is it able to do in these circumstances? What emotions are you experiencing as a result of how your body is responding?*

- Now **put these two reflections side by side** to determine a more complete and composite picture of your life as you long for it to be. (i.e., a *future stage of development your soul is hungering* for and also a *corresponding state of development your body must be in* to fulfill your deepest desires. Write some descriptive phrases about your vision.

Let these exercises set the stage for the optimization of this year's Ramadan. Whenever you are able to identify where you want to be, you can then more specifically discern an appropriate intention and plan for getting there.

Now that you have an image of arriving at a destination that fulfills deep longings within your soul, and have also determined a complementary body condition needed to accomplish this goal, you will need to develop a specific intention and powerful sense of purpose for getting there. First, take time to create a du'a that explicitly petitions Allah's Aid in developing your growing sense of personal purpose and mission. Below is a sample template and example to assist you in framing your du'a based on the insights you received in this exercise.

Ya Allah, from deep within my soul where only You, my Creator have inspired me, I have a powerful longing to

_____.
(What you long to be or do)

So please help me become _____
(The state of health you need to have)

so I can be more productive in my efforts and actions that are pleasing to You, which will empower me as Your servant to make a more meaningful contribution to my family and community

EXAMPLE:
Ya Allah, from deep within my soul, where only You as my Creator have inspired me, I have a powerful longing to establish a thriving and successful business so I can provide the best Islamic education for my children and help pay tuition for other children who want to attend Muslim schools, but can't afford it. So please help me to become free of my diabetes, more clearly focused and full of energy so I can be more productive in my efforts and actions that are pleasing to You, which will empower me as Your servant to make a more meaningful contribution to my family and community.

<u>Exercise:</u>

1. Using the template on pg. 45 as a guide, write your du'a for seeking Allah's Help and His Angels in pursuing your vision.

Chapter 5 – Creating Clearer Intentions for More Powerful Results

Man (mind) can have nothing but what it strives for; and the fruit of
its striving will soon come in sight
Al-Qur'an 53:39-40

Allah is *The* Creator, the *best* to create – who creates from nothing; however man, the human mind, has been given the ingenuity to develop designs and forms from the natural creation based on what Allah has already created. Visioning is a very powerful tool given to the human mind by Allah (SWT). It gives man the ability to clearly and specifically visualize future outcomes we wish to actualize in our personal lives. In fact what we see in the man-made world, at any given time, are manifestations of visions and ideas that were originally inspired in the hearts and minds of men's souls. Therefore, we are creators, too!

Begin launching *your* creative power by framing an intention to actualize the vision you formed in the last chapter.

And, as a Muslim of course, the best way to declare and move forward with your intentions is to develop a concise and articulate du'a that continues to petition Allah for His Help and Guidance in the path of working to achieve what you intend. Turn your intentions into du'as and Allah's Power magnifies your efforts and strivings towards whatever you lawfully desire.

Once intentions are set into motion, they usually become manifest if you are determined to stick with them. There may be many twists and turns on your journey towards achieving your goal, but Allah's Promise is True in fulfilling what is in the heart of the true believer. He will certainly assist you through any doubtful, shaky times that may make it seem unlikely that you will arrive at your destination. This includes getting through circumstances that elicit fear, create distractions, and most assuredly invite opposition from internal and external forces. Your responsibility however, lies in your continued strides at being committed, staying your course and never, ever giving up!

Since your vision projects that you move forward in a more elevated and enlightened manner in doing things that are most pleasing to Allah, should you have any doubt that you will not have His aid and the aid of His Angels as you continue to cry out to Him in du'a to attain this weighty goal? Especially during this Blessed Month, as you endeavor to earn His bountiful rewards through performing the Fast and requisite acts?

What's interesting is that in this modern age where principles in religion and science are often overlapping and affirming each other, many spiritually-based ideas about intentions are being validated by cutting-edge discoveries in modern science. In Surah 33:5 of the

Holy Qur'an, Allah assures us that in spite of our mistakes, what counts are the intentions in our hearts and in Surah 53:39, "that we will get what we strive for." Scientists have now discovered that at the moment intentions are made, minute pattern changes occur in the brain that create new neural pathways which result in information being processed in new ways thus opening up opportunities for new avenues of expression.[4]

In other words, when intentions are stated, Allah has an inherent design within the biology of the human mind that triggers a neurological chain of micro-events which give rise to circumstances that allow you to pursue your intentions in ways you could never have imagined. Even though you may be unable to perfectly execute every task needed to reach your goals, *(there certainly will be times when you mess up or just don't feel like doing what you think, in the moment, needs to be done)*, simply out of your commitment to put your intentions into action, Allah will continue to provide new opportunities for you to gradually step into realizing them. Nonetheless, taking the reins of responsibility to develop a focused plan and strategy for directing your intentions and turning them into dynamic actions is a major factor in determining your ultimate success. In fact, your intellect, your conscious mind, is responsible for planning and strategizing to get what your soul says it needs and wants. The science of the mind and body and how it interacts with the material world is shown in the following life formula (which in pop culture has been referred to as "The Secret"):

Intentions + belief + determined efforts = A manifestation (in the world) of the success you are seeking.

Because of Allah's *Rahmah*, His Beneficence for all of His human creatures, this formula will essentially work for all who follow it. However, when this principle, which is inherent in the basic Plan of how Allah created the universe to operate, is driven by *tauheed* belief (oneness of G-d with no partners and following the life example of His Prophet) and then amplified during Ramadan by surrendering to the Divine Dictates of the prescribed Fast – abstinence of food, drink and lawful sex, plus performing Salat, and the reading and study of Al-Qur'an – the possibilities for sustained blessings and achievement go off the scale. Particularly, when our longings are not spurred by fantasies for self-gratification or self-aggrandizement but are driven by a desire to offer sincere service and contributions as Allah's servant, we can feel confident that our dua's and strivings are being accepted by our Lord and will be fulfilled, insha'Allah.

This intense pursuit of personal development – spiritually, mentally and physically – is what Allah wants for His human servants during Ramadan. That's why He loves the breath of the fasting Muslim. He knows that in our commitment to the Fast and the fasting practices, we are soulfully engaged in the process of developing an elevated consciousness and lifestyle for becoming the khalifah He created and ordained for us to be!

Your physical body is the vehicle or vessel in which the potential for mind-body-soul actualization is to take place. If your body vehicle is weak, in disrepair or significantly compromised, then every other facet of your being functions at less than its true capacity.

However, the physical abstinence of food, drink and lawful sex from dawn to sunset during Ramadan is a critical tool that aligns and cleanses the body to optimize usage of the three essential nutrients that best sustain our lives – water, food and oxygen. Learning and developing strategies to take in high quality and appropriate quantities of these natural elements on a daily basis will pave the way to creating a strong physical foundation on which your intellectual and spiritual faculties can be best formed and expressed.

In the next chapter you will be given information to begin planning your personal strategies for optimizing your health before, during and after Ramadan by seeking to create an alignment of your body, mind and soul.

Exercise:
1. Articulate the intentions you have for pursuing your vision. What actions do you need to carry out? What first steps will you take?

2. Write a du'a that expresses what you intend to do and which petitions Allah for His Help in committing to your actions.

Chapter 6 – Water, the Phenomenal Fluid

We made from water every living thing.
Al-Qur'an 21:30

Water is the essence of life. In fact water, within itself, is a living entity. It is moving energy from which all life comes and all life needs in order to sustain their vital life processes. The human body needs water to metabolize fat, remove waste from cells, and keep our brains healthy.   Essentially water allows communication between our different organs and facilitates the flow of oxygen, nutrients and energy via the 60,000 miles of blood vessels that run throughout our body.

Yet as critical as water is to existence, it's possible that you are in the ranks of the chronically dehydrated *(along with over 75% of Americans)* and that your body is functioning at a severe deficit in what is needed to simply maintain healthy cells, tissues and organs; all of which leads to systemic breakdown, dysfunction and dis-ease.

> When the body *lacks water* its blood thickens, which consequently impedes circulation. As a result, excess body waste keeps storing in the interstitial space that surrounds the cells. If unresolved, the toxins accumulate and the interstitial space becomes an acidic wasteland that lacks nutrition and proper oxygenation. Because of this, the cells there become abnormal. In order to survive, these cells have to rely on fermentation processes instead of oxidative functions. This fermenting condition will eventually lead to cancer or other degenerative diseases like Parkinson's and Alzheimer's.[5]

However well you might know that you need it, you may still find it difficult to drink – pure water that is! Most people would rather drink sodas, juices, milk, coffees or flavored and sweetened waters – anything but plain "tasteless" water. Yet it's only when water has nothing added to it that it really quenches thirst and in turn purifies and cleanses your body. On the other hand, the high sugar content in sodas and flavored drinks pulls water out of cells rather than putting water into them thus triggering or intensifying dehydration.

What if the lakes, rivers and oceans were filled with liquids other than pure water – perhaps even some you frequently drink? Can you imagine a lake of orange juice, a stream of coffee or an ocean of grape soda? Think about the gooey stickiness and residue that would be in the areas surrounding these waterways. Envision the aquatic life (plants and fish) that would be struggling to survive within these thick, sugary liquids. Can you picture your body organs trying to stay healthy and functional in such a toxic environment? But that's exactly what is happening when you continuously consume drinks other than the miraculous fluid Allah gave you for natural cleansing and hydration.

Like so many people these days, you've probably convinced yourself that you don't like water. *"It doesn't taste good or it doesn't taste like anything. I just can't stand to drink plain water."* If this is what you believe, then your mind is feeding you a perception that is a lie. You are designed in your natural fitra (the original nature that Allah created you in) to automatically want that which gives you life!

Not to want water, certainly is to invite death (on some level), which no healthy-minded person will say is their aim. When you tell yourself you don't want water and/or that you don't like it, you're hearing untruths that are products of delusional thoughts in your mind. These delusional thoughts may come via the media which is trying to sell you all types of flavored drinks and convince you that they're good for you as well as the influences of people in your life who did not place a value on drinking water when you were growing up. And, those who do not place a value on it now.

The body needs extra hydration, particularly when fasting. Not only does water quench the deep thirst of a fasting believer and perform all of the vital functions identified above, but water also helps to flush additional impurities that are broken down in the body through the fasting process. Drinking pure water will help alleviate the symptoms of detoxification such as headaches, tiredness, irritability and joint pain.

Get in the habit of drinking pure water now so your body can already be well-hydrated before the Fast in order to maximize its potential to be at its best when it begins to deal with the rigors of the fasting regimen. Having difficulty getting started? The following exercise and recommended strategies can help.

Water Visualization Exercise:

To increase your value and appreciation for water and to intensify your awareness of it to maintain your existence, do this short exercise for some deep reflection.

- Take 3 deep breaths to focus and ground your attention on your beautiful human form.

- Reflect on the reality that your body is comprised of over 75% water. Seek to connect your personal reservoir of water to the world's rivers, streams, and vast oceans. Include in your reflection the mist that hovers over the lakes, the cloudbursts that rain down from the skies, the springs that bubble up from the earth and the condensation that's visible in the morning dew. Sensitize yourself to feel a bond with all of this water.

- Ponder on the gift of water. Say to yourself, "No life can come forth or be sustained without it . . . my life began in water and in order to continue to be healthy I must consume quality amounts of it."

- Reflect on water's soothing coolness and its ability to quench your thirst as it slowly trickles down your waiting throat. Reflect on its journey as it goes throughout your body carrying nutrients to your cells and moving poisons to be flushed out of your system.

- Think about the relief you feel for being able to drink it at the end of a long day of fasting. Connect with the feeling that water gives you of life, freshness and vitality.

- For a brief moment, consider how life looks when deprived of water. Think of deserts, drooping flowers and dried up leaves and think of how you feel and look when you don't drink enough water. Perhaps you're tired, skin eruptions may occur, dark circles may appear under your eyes and/or you develop a headache that won't quit.

- Be grateful for all this water (both outside and inside of you) that surrounds your life. Make a du'a of appreciation and thankfulness.

- Make a commitment to never again deny this miraculous gift from entering your body. Vow to drink it willingly and abundantly!

PREPARE for Quality Hydration Before Ramadan

Again, it's best to get in the habit of drinking water right away rather than wait for Ramadan to begin. Now is the time to start toning down the "other drinks" you consume and revving up the volume of water you consume. Most importantly, you must adjust your mindset to make it your beverage of choice. Also, if you're experiencing Ramadan in the dead heat of summer or in a climate with high temperatures in the winter, you want to have your body well-hydrated before you're forced to curtail your drinking during the daylight hours. You want to be well-accustomed to having an established rhythm of drinking water prior to the start of Ramadan so that it will be easier to tweak your drinking schedule at that time rather than trying to begin one.

How much water to drink daily? A good rule of thumb is to drink ½ your weight in ounces. So if you weigh 140 lbs. you would drink 70 oz. and if you weigh 250 lbs. you would drink 125 oz. (almost a full gallon). During hot weather or when you're being highly active you may need to drink more. Also, if you are eating plenty of fresh green, leafy vegetables (not canned or frozen) or fresh fruits (particularly melons) you may not need to drink quite as much. Get into the habit of listening to your body to determine its needs but don't use thirst as an indicator for when to drink water. It's said that when you *feel* thirst, your body is already in the beginning stages of dehydration.

What type of water should you drink? This question asked of anyone born over 50 years ago would have seemed ridiculous and met with a look of amazement and a response, *"Water is just water, what do you mean what type?"* But of course we know in today's world much of the water we drink originates from many varied sources (wells, springs, lakes, reservoirs) and is bottled at facilities sometimes hundreds or thousands of miles away.

Over the years, many "spinoffs" of water have also emerged. Vitamin water, flavored water, seltzer water, smart water, and so on. All of these choices can be quite confusing unless you remember to simply seek out plain water -- *not flavored, sweetened, or containing any additives . . . just plain water.* It may be spring, distilled, alkaline or filtered water. Actually there are theories and rational justifications for drinking or not drinking each of these types of water, however, the best advice is to get a quality water filter so you're not constantly paying out of pocket for bottled water (which can total hundreds of dollars a year) and so you're not contributing to pollution of the environment with non-biodegradable plastics. Many health practitioners tout the benefits of alkaline water, but if you are conscientious about eating an alkaline diet (which is not hard to do if you are committed to eating an abundance of plant-based foods) then the expense of investing in an alkaline water filtration system is not really needed or warranted.

What you want to avoid doing, if at all possible, is drinking water directly from your tap (without filtering it) as city water usually has chemicals added to it. Keep in mind however, that it's better to drink tap water than no water at all if that's all that is available or that you can afford. Allah has created your body with an amazing amount of resiliency to be able to persevere under less than optimum conditions including the ability to process and eliminate low levels of toxins that are likely to be present in tap water. However, your body won't survive or maintain any level of quality health for long without a sufficient supply of water to meet the demands of its vital functions.

Though you certainly want to put the highest quality possible of everything in your body, if you can't afford to pay for bottled water or a water filter, then drink what is available. Your body needs water . . . . period, paragraph! If you must drink tap water then do so for as short a period as possible and place a priority in saving money to purchase a treatment device or system that will provide you with a higher quality of water. Also, in some areas of the country *(usually rural or small towns)* tap water can have a high standard of purity because its source may be a local well or reservoir fed by an underground spring. Therefore, investigate and research water options that are best for you and your family.

How to drink the amount of water you need? By the time most people experience a feeling of thirst; their bodies are already registering a water deficit indicating some level of dehydration. Consequently, it is very important that you are aware of how much your body really needs, otherwise you may not drink nearly enough simply because you rarely feel thirsty throughout the day.

Also, you may have to develop a strong resolve to develop the habit of drinking *pure water,* especially if you're used to reaching for "other beverages" that you favor first. But nonetheless it can be done. Again, reflect on the meaning of water in life and its purpose – and the appreciation and gratitude to Allah (SWT) we should have for giving us water. *Which of the Favors of your Lord will you deny?*

Take time to develop a consciousness for being attuned to your individual symptoms when you don't have enough water in your system. Tired? Headache? Joints inflamed? Pimples on your skin, circles under your eyes, darkened urine or constipated? These latter three are serious indications that you have been without water for quite a while and your body is at a deficit.

Here's a suggested strategy to start getting enough water in your system on a daily basis.

- Get a **16 oz. or 20 oz. glass** and designate it as *your* water glass. It's far easier to drink a few larger containers throughout the day than to drink a lot of smaller ones. In other words, rather than drink *eight* 10 oz. glasses to get 80 oz. of water throughout your day, why not drink *four* 20 oz. glasses or *five* 16 oz. glasses?

- Also, it is very helpful to schedule designated times to drink water. Example: to get in 80 oz. of water using a 20 oz. cup, schedule your water drinking at 6AM (right before or after Fajr), 10 am, 2 pm and 6 pm. It's best not to drink water too late in the evening so it won't disrupt your sleep by having to get up to use the bathroom.

- Another trick for getting the water habit under your belt is to use a timer. Select your designated times for drinking your water and use your cell phone or alarm clock as a reminder for when to get your next glass.

- A simpler system for the above strategy would be to drink a glass of water (in your designated container) before or after each Salat! ☺

- Don't drink water while eating because it can dilute stomach juices and digestive enzymes. Water temporarily causes less production of stomach acid and therefore can interfere with digestion of food especially protein. It is best to drink water by itself at least 5 – 10 minutes before a meal or *preferably* 30 minutes prior to a meal to allow for better digestion and maximum absorption of nutrients from your food. For the same reasons it is also best not to drink water or any liquid for 30 minutes or an hour *after* you have eaten.

- **Remember.** Drinking pure water is essential. Water should flow through your body like a river running through land picking up impurities and carrying them out to sea.

MAINTAIN Quality Hydration During Ramadan

Of course you can't consume water *during* the hours of fasting so how do you get it all in? First of all, if you've spent a few weeks before Ramadan establishing a water routine where you're getting sufficient amounts of water, then your body will have been well hydrated by now and you won't be at a deficit. You'll be able to sustain the rigors of the Fast much better, particularly during a high heat period. Cutting back on water intake while you're fasting (because you won't have time to do drink as much) won't be as detrimental as if you'd not established a good water regimen prior to Ramadan.

However, I suggest you use the power of visualization and intentions to reach a goal of drinking as close to the amount of water you were drinking before Ramadan as possible. Keep in mind a vision of how you feel and look when you've been getting enough water in your system. By now, if you've been successful in increasing your water intake, you should be noticing changes in your energy level (water is a powerful energizer), your flexibility and fluidity of movement (water "oils" your joints), the appearance of your skin (water gives a youthful radiant glow) and a host of other benefits.

If you have not yet reached a level of visible success in drinking water, then use this list of **water drinking benefits** to create a picture of how you plan to feel and look after routinely drinking the daily quota for your weight and activity level:

- Triggers weight loss – appetite suppressant and flushes body of toxins
- Eliminates headaches

- Creates youthful appearance with healthy skin
- Increases alertness and focus for better productivity
- Increases energy for more stamina during exercise
- Aids with digestion and constipation
- Lubricates muscles and joints
- Boosts immune system
- Relieves fatigue and exhaustion
- Improves mood
- Reduces cancer risks (can dilute concentration of cancer-causing agents)

Now, simply make an intention for the amount of water you will drink before and after the Fast each day. Again **use a strategy for scheduling the times** that you will drink it. Suggested schedule:

- Drink a glass right after rising for suhoor (meal before dawn).
- Drink another glass a few minutes after eating suhoor.
- Break your Fast with a full glass of water. Sip, do not gulp, so that your stomach doesn't cramp. Don't be tempted to drink any liquid other than water at this time. The body essentially needs water and water *only* after it has been deprived of it for the majority of your waking hours.
- Drink another glass of water later after completing your Iftar meal.
- If you still have the desire to consume one of the "other beverages" then squeeze in a small amount between drinking water. Establish drinking water as one of the pillars upholding the hardiness of your physical health. Don't give leeway to anything that will get in the

way of drinking the amount you need. Otherwise the crumbling of this one pillar alone may cause your house (i.e. body) to come tumbling down.

- o Note that during those first days of the Fast you may experience ailments such as headaches, joint pain, constipation, foggy thinking or even cold-like symptoms (which may be triggered by the effects of detoxification that come from fasting). Drinking sufficient water before and after the hours of fasting, will make them miraculously disappear.

- o A word of caution; remember that it is absolutely necessary to be well-hydrated during the Fast when weather temperatures are very high. If you experience symptoms of *heat exhaustion* or *heat stroke*[6], break your Fast immediately and drink water. Make up the day later.

SUSTAIN Quality Hydration After Ramadan

Certainly, if you have been successful in cultivating a routine of drinking your body's needed quota of water before and during Ramadan it should not be difficult to continue after Ramadan. By now you should have acquired a genuine taste and appreciation for drinking water and are beginning to prefer it over other type beverages. It's not to say that you can't also drink juices (please make them 100% natural) or sometimes an occasional soda (natural, too!) or an even more occasional milkshake or cappuccino. Herbal teas, which have high water content, can be drunk more frequently as long as you don't load them with additional sweeteners.

Yet, and still, plain water with *nothing* added (except perhaps a slight twist of lemon or lime) is your best line of offense and defense in maintaining proper hydration and flushing your body of daily toxins.

Keep water in front of you throughout the day. Carry your designated glass or container with you and keep it full so you are reminded to drink it rather than get distracted with other things competing for your attention. Always keep in mind the amount of water that your body needs based on your weight, the weather and your level of activity.

Remember to drink water before succumbing to a seeming uncontrollable urge to run to the vending machine at work or stop at a convenience store to quickly sweep up a candy bar or bag of chips. Sudden hunger is often a signal that is a misinterpretation of what your body really needs; usually which is something other than food. Sometimes what your body is *really* saying is that it needs more hydration. Water will be most gratifying in such instances and can significantly curb your desire to eat or drink substances that may not be best for you.

As the weather gets colder towards the winter months, the desire to drink water may become more difficult, even for those who have developed a comfort level in drinking it on a regular basis. Don't try to drink cold water straight from the refrigerator at this time. In fact, some health experts say very cold water should never be drank as its temperature can be too shocking and extreme for your internal system. For the most part, water at room temperature or that's mildly cool is your best drinking alternative throughout the year. Yet, deciding to drink or to not drink cold water can be considered a bio-individual choice, not a hard fast rule. During the winter months, if you have a natural aversion to cold water, then try drinking it at room temperature or even heat it and drink it hot like a tea. This can be surprisingly satisfying and will guarantee your continued hydration throughout the winter when bodies have an even greater tendency to dry out because of lengthy exposure to artificial heat.

<u>Reflection:</u>

1. What do you notice about yourself when you don't drink enough water – dark circles under your eyes, skin eruptions, bad breath, dark urine, headaches or something else?

2. How do you visualize yourself looking and feeling as a result of drinking enough water every day?

3. Based on your body weight how much water should you be drinking each day? _____ oz.

4. How many ounces does your designated container hold? _____ oz.

5. How many containers do you need to drink daily to achieve your quota_____?

6. Do you need to drink extra water because of weather or intense activity? If yes, how much more? _____ Total _____ oz.

7. What strategy did you develop for drinking the amount of water your body needs every day before, during and after Ramadan?

Chapter 7 – Air, the Bountiful Breath

And We send the fertilizing winds . . .
Holy Qur'an 15:22

Oxygen is another life-giving, vital element in nature that is a gift from Allah (SWT) and due to the unique atmosphere of our planet and the vast greenery that covers the earth, we are surrounded by it at every step of our lives. People don't usually think of oxygen being an essential nutrient for the human body, but it certainly is.

Oxygen helps to nourish and metabolize the body just like any food substance. In fact it is considered the single most important substance taken into the body; *"oxygen nourishes the cells, it provides the energy needed to metabolize carbohydrates, it allows chemical transport, breaks down waste products and toxins, regulates the pH of body chemistry, drives the desire to breathe, and fights hostile organisms. Oxygen is the undisputed king of body chemistry, and as such is your body's most important nutrient!"*[7]

That being said, oxygen is even more critical to our existence than water or food. A person can live 8 - 14 days without water, 4 – 8 weeks without food, but only a few minutes without a sufficient supply of air. Because oxygen is in abundance in the atmosphere, barring some catastrophe, accident or illness that leaves us oxygen deprived, it would seem unlikely we need worry about getting enough of it. But that's only partially true.

Before you breathe your last breath in this life, you will have inhaled and exhaled about 100 million times. Though you breathe in enough oxygen for your body to survive, more than likely you are not inhaling large enough quantities so it can thrive! Breathing in deeper quantities of air on a regular basis is critical to elevating physical health and producing calm, clear thinking and focus. It is the conscious movement of breath throughout the body by deeply inhaling and exhaling that creates a state of relaxed vitality for more optimal levels of health to be realized and sustained.

Training the breath is a tool to achieving heightened energy and awareness. The practice of deep breathing reintegrates the body, mind and soul and releases a vast reserve of energy already within you that can generate greater unity and peace. The practice of deep breathing allows you to be alive every moment, naturally. Breath is life!

To deep breathe means simply to inhale your breath all the way into your abdominal region – right below your belly button which in traditional Chinese martial arts is called your *dantien*. Deep breathing in this way oxygenates your body and sends this much needed nutrient to areas throughout your system to increase energy flow and eliminate blockages that cause tension, pain and can lead to dis-ease. As a result, deep breathing relieves stress, decreases pain and helps to purify the body of toxins that can lead to all types of sickness. Stopping to take a few deep breaths during the day can make all the difference in the world regarding how you feel physically, emotionally, mentally and spiritually.

More than likely Prophet Muhammad and most people in earlier parts of history were habitual deep breathers. It is generally thought that the faster pace of modern life has quickened the average breathing rate so that most people's inhalations are very shallow – reaching no further than their lungs. This type of breathing is called thoracic or chest breathing and causes continuous constriction of the muscles in the upper body and stomach so that people are chronically tense and stressed. This habitual tension, one of the primary triggers in the current rise in dis-ease, can be dispelled simply by engaging in a few rounds of deep breathing which create a calming effect throughout the entire body.

In Prophet Muhammad's (saw) regular trips to the Cave to meditate, his breathing probably slowed even more as he went into a deeper reflective state. When you find a quiet space where you can empty your mind of racing thoughts, your breathing will settle into a natural rhythm that synchronizes with the slowing down of your mental activity. Amazingly as your breath slows down, your mental *acuity* becomes sharper, giving you more clarity of thought as you reflect on key personal issues and challenges with an increasing laser-like focus. You have now entered into *your* "cave".

PREPARE for Quality Breathing Before Ramadan

Breathing into your lungs is regarded as shallow breathing and is the type of breathing most people do by default without thinking about it. When under stress your breath gets even more shallow and rapid, hindering much needed oxygen from flowing through your system. Because you are accustomed to breathing in this way day in and day out, beginning to cultivate a pattern of deep breathing will take focused commitment and determination.

However, the best way to start deep breathing is to just do it. Find a technique you feel is simple and fits the style that makes you feel most comfortable. Some deep breathing instructors recommend sitting up, others recommend lying down. Some recommend breathing through the nose only while others recommend the mouth only. Some say to alternate between nose and mouth. The style really doesn't matter; again, whatever makes you comfortable. What is important is that you learn how to use some type of breathing technique to get more oxygen into your body and that you promise yourself to practice it regularly.

Though it may seem that all that's needed to get started is to simply breathe in more air, deep breathing works best by "measuring" the breath, meaning to count as you inhale and exhale. When you count your breath it increases your concentration and helps to calibrate your breath into a rhythmic pattern. To begin, try breathing in to a count of two and exhaling to a count of four and over time working up to an inhale of four or six and an exhale of eight or twelve. Remember to release your breath long and slowly, expelling all air until you can't breathe out any more. In this way your contracted abdomen naturally breathes in the next breath and will generate vitality, giving a sense of fullness and energy to the body. As this happens, your mind, along with your body, will relax.

Here is a simple exercise you can begin:

1. Lie on your back or stand or sit comfortably and place your hands on your stomach (abdomen).
2. Inhale slowly and deeply, letting your abdomen expand like a balloon. (Keep a hand on your stomach as you feel it expanding.)
3. Let your abdomen fall as you exhale slowly; you are releasing old, stale air full of toxins.
4. Inhale slowly again and make sure you are pressing the air all the way out each time you exhale.
5. Repeat this breathing cycle for as long as possible. You may only be able to comfortably do this for 2 – 3 minutes at first, but gradually seek to increase the time.

To gain in-depth knowledge regarding deep breathing, Google the topic or search for a YouTube video to view different styles being demonstrated. Most techniques are very simple and learning the basics only takes a few minutes, but quality deep breathing is learned over time.

Here's another very simple breathing exercise you can do that will balance and invigorate your energy in a very short span of time:

1. Use right thumb to close off right nostril.
2. Inhale slowly through left nostril

3. Pause for a second
4. Now close left nostril with right fore-finger and release thumb off right nostril
5. Exhale through your right nostril
6. Now, inhale through right nostril
7. Pause
8. Use thumb to close off right nostril
9. Breathe out through left nostril
10. This is one round. Start slowly with 1 or 2 rounds and gradually increase. Never force. Sit quietly for a few moments after you have finished.

Leading up to Ramadan simply choose a deep breathing technique and seek to practice it diligently so it becomes easier and easier to get into a relaxed state by taking in a few breaths. Deep breathing once or twice a day for 3 -5 minutes is a good start. Maybe even less time when you first begin. The strategy is to start within your comfort zone and gradually challenge your endurance and level of difficulty as you go along.

MAINTAIN Quality Breathing During Ramadan

Deep breathing can come in handy during Ramadan to center and focus you while you are fasting, making Salat and reading the Qur'an. The deep breathing pattern is naturally relaxing, slows down your thinking, and will place you in a more reflective state. More information can be absorbed and your connection with the Divine Presence (of Allah's Ruh and His Angels) can be heightened with greater sensitivity and awareness. Deep breathing is a great enhancer of the fasting experience.

Deep breathing can be done when first waking and in doing so will improve your digestive capability at suhoor, filling your stomach with enough oxygen to better assimilate, absorb and transport the nutrients in your food to where they're needed in your body. You can also deep breathe as you're making salat. This is not a suggestion for bidah (i.e. innovating a new way of worship), but simply a recommendation to take deeper, slower breaths as you recite Qur'an and move from one position to another which will keep you from rushing through your prayer and will significantly enhance your consciousness and awareness as you commune with your Lord.

Also, when you are in intense discourse with your Lord during the Night of Power, you can use deep breathing as a key tool for boosting your physical, mental and spiritual energy; thus affording you an opportunity for receiving deeper levels of personal inspiration and guidance throughout this very special night. Breathing deeply will center you, give you greater focus and assist you in becoming better attuned to an inner listening for comprehending deeper insights.

Imam Salim Mumin, Arabic instructor and founder of the Muslim American Logic Institute (MALI), also offers this profound insight regarding deep breathing:

> "As you recite the Qur'an in its original Arabic tongue, the long and short vowel intonations of the words and the varying pauses throughout the recitation will naturally cause you to breathe in a slower more rhythmic pattern. Deepening of the breath will occur automatically if you keep a steady smooth pace. And, as you take time to reflect on the metaphors and deeper meanings of Qur'an throughout the pauses, an intense calm and peace may descend within you. Also, with proper intonation of the Arabic words their sound vibrations resonate throughout your body and can produce a healing impact . . . *Riyadah*, an Arabic term usually associated with sports, literally means religious exercise, so the act of reading Qur'an in Arabic and the deep breathing it produces are forms of *riyadah*, a beneficial exercise that reflects worship of Allah and enhances the body, mind and soul."[8]

SUSTAIN Quality Breathing After Ramadan

Sustaining deep breathing as a regular practice in your life can make a big difference in your level of health. It will reduce your daily stress and continue to give you a calm focused approach to challenges and problems that you face. Start your day with deep breathing and end it with deep breathing. And throughout your day take pauses between your work to engage in a few rounds of deep cleansing breaths that will focus, center, and give you more mental clarity in whatever you are doing.

You may find it difficult to pinpoint a time and space to practice deep breathing. Here are a few tips to allow you to fit it into your schedule no matter how busy you are:

1. **Reflect on what deep breathing can do for your health** and decide that it's something important you need to do on a regular basis; then make your intentions. Say a du'a and be committed to finding a way to make it happen.

2. **Remember, deep breathing is a very flexible activity.** You only need a few minutes to get a regular practice started and to benefit. When you can, expand the time you devote to it and cut back when you have less time.

3. **Look for a few moments in your daily schedule** when you're already by yourself instead of trying to push things aside to create time. Malikah Karim, yoga instructor recommends associating your deep breathing practice with something you normally do on a regular basis every day, i.e. brushing your teeth or right after you make one or more of your salat.

Malikah, also says, "Know that you don't have to be in the "perfect" environment to have a good space for deep breathing. Just find a place where you can be alone with no interruptions for a few minutes. You may need to retreat into the bathroom or go sit in your car for a deep breather. Remember all that is needed is a few minutes or less for this practice. Perhaps, just one minute. There're a lot of breaths in one minute!"[9]

Aqiylah Collins, a health coach and Reiki master encourages her clients to, "go out in nature where just being there inclines you to breathe deeply. You naturally want to inhale the goodness of your surroundings and all the greenery around you gives you such a vast supply of oxygen!"[10]

Take a class that incorporates deep breathing as part of the workout or regimen, i.e. yoga, qigong or tai chi. Malikah teaches a type of yoga called Vinyasa that aligns breath and movement, merging them into a dynamic dance of energy. She says the synergistic effect produced from this complementary action between breath and body leads to improved health and healing, particularly for women who many times "have let societal pressures take their breath away!" Another type of yoga that incorporates deep breathing as a central focus is Kundalini. Qigong and Tai chi, other ancient exercise art forms, offer similar benefits and methods of synchronizing movement with breath.

Also, teach other family members to be deep breathers. Practice deep breathing while you pray, eat, walk, work and sit. You'll be amazed at the transformation that you'll undergo. It will help you minimize stress, emotional upsets, mood swings and bursts of anger. You'll find it easier to live and practice your Deen than ever before. Deep breathers who regularly read the Holy Qur'an and perform Salat can advance a community a long way!

Reflection:

1. What technique do you feel most comfortable using to deep breathe?

2. How do you feel after a few cycles of deep breathing?

3. In what ways are you most looking forward to deep breathing benefiting your life – reducing tension, calming your body, helping you to sleep, increasing focus or . . . ?

4. How many times are you committed to engage in deep breathing during the course of your day?

Chapter 8 - Food, the Vital Substances

Eat what is on the earth lawful and good.
Holy Qur'an 2:168

A very large portion of each waking day is spent interacting with food or the thought of food in some way. Buying it, preparing it, eating it at meals, snacking on it between meals; sometimes eating too much of it, feeling guilty about eating too much of it; sneaking it, denying it, loving it, hating it. Yet simply out of commitment, love and obedience to our Creator, Allah (SWT) we are able to restrain ourselves from consuming *any* food for over half of our waking hours every day during the month of Ramadan. This ability to Fast consistently for 29 or 30 days from dawn to sunset is a sign of the great potential we have for achieving self-restraint in all other areas of our lives.

The Fast, though very demanding, may for some believers, be the easiest part of the injunctions given by Allah to adhere to during the month (particularly for veteran fasters). Certainly, reading a thirtieth of the Qur'an every day can be equally or more daunting than going without food or drink and making each and every Salat on time as well as supererogatory prayers can be quite challenging. Yet countless numbers of Muslims throughout the world rise to the occasion during this Blessed Month and not only complete each day of fasting through proper abstinence from food, but also complete their reading of the Holy Qur'an and make their 5 daily prayers during the course of the day, as well as perform many rak'ats of Tarawih Salat after 'Isha every night before going to bed.

However, one aspect of the Fast many Muslims fall down on and have yet to master are the regulations regarding the *amount* and the *types* of food they should be consuming prior to beginning and ending their Fast each day. But what you put into your body *before* and *after* your daily Fast is very critical because the physical process of fasting induces the body to start cleansing and purifying itself. So, is it rational to engage rigorously in the practice of fasting, which is detoxifying your body, and then break your Fast with foods that are returning toxins back into your body? Think about it!

Consequently, the goal should be that the two daily meals you are permitted to eat during Ramadan – Suhoor and Iftar – consist of foods which are not only best for you but are eaten in moderation. Eating in this manner will result in proper digestion so the nutrients in the foods you consume can be maximized by your body. When asked how much a faster should eat when beginning or breaking their Fast for the day, the Prophet (SAW) stated, *"Eat the meal of a poor man."* Thus, the foods you choose to eat, how much of them you eat and the manner in which you eat them requires using great discernment.

Reflect on the purpose of food. Food is energy – it is a form of energy as is every entity in the universe. Yet food (substances on this planet that are designated by Allah for human consumption) is specifically intended to *add* energy or augment existing energy within the human form. So the purpose of food is, first and foremost, to provide you with energy and to sustain your energy. So, if after an hour or two of eating you do not feel a rise in your energy level or you find your energy lagging before the end of the day, then more than likely this is due to the type and amount of food you're eating, as well as the way in which it's being eaten.

Just as a man-made machine or device requires some type of fuel as an energy source to function, the human body also needs fuel to function. Food is our fuel. And, not just any type of food can be used as fuel; it must be high quality food. Low quality foods will not provide what your body needs. You must consume essential amounts of vitamins, minerals, fiber, proteins, fats and carbohydrates on a daily basis in order for them to be effectively and efficiently metabolized, absorbed and distributed throughout your system for healthy function of your bodily organs.

However, are you one who invests in high octane gasoline for your beautiful car, but purchases cheap fuel (i.e. processed food) for your beautiful body? Yet, what you get from high octane gas – improved performance and mileage for your car – is the same as what you will get for your body when you eat high quality foods. What are high quality foods? High quality foods are those that are whole, natural and often times labeled organic.[11]

Quality foods (that Allah has intended for human consumption for optimal growth and development) grow naturally from the earth and are not altered in any harmful way before they reach you. No long names or lists of ingredients are needed to tell you what's in them. In fact, in most cases they don't require special packaging or labeling because what you see is what you get.

Any fresh, natural fruits or vegetables that have been harvested from plants that grow from the ground and *have not* been put into a box, can or container of any kind are usually going to be quality foods. If they have been placed into any packaged form then that means that these "grow foods" (natural foods grown from the ground) have made a detour and been taken to a factory where more than likely they have been stripped of essential nutrients – and artificial ingredients with preservatives, refined sugars and salts have been added, thus rendering them highly toxic and dangerous to your health.

However, in today's high-tech media climate where information about any and everything is easily accessible, you probably already know this. Who hasn't seen the latest TV show or read the latest article touting the benefits of healthy foods and stating which ones to stay away from? In this regard, Americans are said to be the most well-informed people on Earth regarding what is required to achieve and maintain good health.   Yet, we are also the *most unhealthy* people, suffering with higher chronic dis-ease rates than any other industrialized nation.

There is a disconnect between what most Americans know about health and what they practice. This is occurring not only among "other people" in the society, but also among Muslims. Despite having the best Book, the Holy Qur'an, and the best example in Prophet Muhammad (saw) for every aspect of living including how to eat, we are witnessing obesity, diabetes, hypertension, arthritis and cancer as common illnesses existing in our communities. There is even a rise, in recent years, of Alzheimer's, Parkinson's and other neurological disturbances among Muslims.

What do all these illnesses have to do with food? More than you may think. According to former U.S. Surgeon General, Dr. C. Everett Koop, of the 2.4 million deaths that occur annually in the US, at least 75% are the result of nutritional and lifestyle factors that are avoidable. Many believing Muslims, who know that nothing happens except by the Qadr (Decree) of Allah, dismiss this information and say that only Allah causes death and no matter what, we will die at the time appointed for us. While this is certainly true, Allah also gives us an intellect and limited free will, which grants us the ability to determine the *quality* of life we live and may even determine the *condition* in which we die.

Yes, you are already decreed to die at a certain pre-determined time, but must you die from cancer or complications from diabetes or some other disease related to the types of food you consume or the lifestyle you've chosen? Perhaps with other choices available to you, your transition from this life can be less devastating; without suffering or burdening others with your continued care. Perhaps you may die quietly in your sleep or from an acute illness you absolutely have no control over, but until then you will have lived a healthy, quality driven, productive life free of dis-ease because of your healthy choices. What if . . . ? Can you envision this rich possibility?

Many people believe aging and sickness are synonymous, but this is not necessarily true. You can live to a ripened age of 80, 90 or more and still have energy, vibrancy and the ability to work and contribute to life. Alhamdulillah, there are quite a few examples of aging octogenarians, nonagenarians and even older believers in our communities who fit this description. If questioned, you would find many of them have cut way back on their food intake and are also very careful of what and when they eat.

Quality food is essential for sustaining the high powered, long-lasting quality life you envision for making a worthy contribution to life that is pleasing to Allah (SWT). There is no better time than Ramadan to modify your present eating habits and develop healthier ones that can be carried forward as a lifelong practice. But to effectively improve your eating habits during Ramadan, as with drinking more water and deep breathing, it is best to prepare *before* the Fast begins.

PREPARE for Quality Eating Before Ramadan

Again, the biggest challenge for many believers during Ramadan is not abstaining from food for long hours, but in choosing the best foods when breaking the Fast and ensuring not to overeat. Overeating is a nemesis that is very difficult to tame once Ramadan begins since the feeling of hunger can be overwhelming when you've abstained from food for over half your waking hours. For most people, it's actually easier to stop eating completely than to cut back on how much food they're eating after they get started. Once salivary glands are triggered, it can be very easy to lose self-control! To curtail this likelihood, the best time to start disciplining your food intake and eating habits is at least a few weeks before Ramadan.

Start now to reduce the amount of food being consumed at meals. Sound too much like a diet? Not intended. Don't count calories or rigidly restrict your food choices or exercise "portion control" by doling out fist-sized helpings onto your plate. The alternative? As opposed to what your appetite (many times falsely stimulated) tells you that you need, conduct an "experiment" over the next few weeks to learn how much food your body *really* needs to satisfy your *genuine* hunger.

The first thing to do is to *slow down* your eating. In fact, let *"slow down"* be your inner mantra in just about everything you do. Stop rushing around every day, doing, doing, doing . . . and seek a slower pace so you have time to connect with what's within. This way you will be able to better connect with the messages your body is constantly sending – which is very important in learning to not overeat. Begin by taking a few deep breaths before you sit down to eat a meal. [Also it was a sunnah practice of Prophet Mohammed to sit while eating a meal.] Not standing or eating on the run is essential; doing either will keep your food from digesting properly. If you are really serious about cutting back on the amount of food you're eating, upon completing your deep breathing, drink a glass of water before beginning your meal.

Also, before you touch any portion of the food you're about to eat, grace your meal with at least *bismillah;* better yet recite Al-Fatihah, the opening surah of the Holy Qur'an. In addition, it would also be good to include a few sincere words reflecting appreciation and awareness for the food Allah has blessed to be on your plate and the process that took place for it to arrive there. After all, it could certainly be otherwise. This may sound cliché-ish or patronizing (not intended) but many people around the world have only a fraction of the food that is available to you, and a sizeable number have nothing at all to eat. So yes, think of all the poor, starving people in the world and be grateful for every morsel in front of you. Doing this alone and doing so sincerely, may help you cut down on the amount of food you eat as you contemplate, empathize and sensitively connect with those who have far less.

Now, as you begin to eat, chew *very, very* slowly. This may be somewhat difficult depending on the habit of chewing that you've cultivated through the years. Most Americans chew fast; which complements their fast-paced lifestyle. Additionally, the propensity to multi-task while eating has become a popular trend. You may be one who talks on the phone, reads a book, watches TV or a movie or engages in heavy conversations while sitting at the table eating, just so you feel you're making "good use" of your "down time". I used to see eating as a very boring, passive activity that needed to be supplemented with more interesting and "engaging" tasks (i.e. reading, talking, looking at TV) to compensate for the "lost" time I felt was being spent sitting and consuming food.

Nothing could be further from the truth. Eating is certainly a worthy activity in and of itself and you are not meant to indulge in it passively. To the contrary, the process of eating is to be actively and consciously engaged in because it requires focused effort to correctly chew for proper digestion as well as maintain a state of mental and emotional calm so digestion can be optimized. If you eat while tense, food will sit in your stomach far longer than needed and putrefy, thereby producing high levels of toxins. This situation is worsened if you eat processed foods which have high levels of toxins to begin with.

Put your focused mind on eating slowly, thoroughly coating your food with saliva, a necessary enzyme needed to begin breaking your food down before it starts its transit into your digestive tract. Remember, digestion begins in the mouth. Just following this simple rule will begin to minimize or eliminate any digestive upsets you may be prone to such as heartburn, acid reflux or even constipation. As you chew your food more slowly, you will become acutely aware of its true flavor, texture and taste and the act of eating itself will become more pleasurable.

If what you're eating is not pleasurable and you're not enjoying it, then it's probably the wrong food (i.e., processed foods with artificial ingredients, refined sugars, salts and chemicals). Should this be the case, then by chewing more slowly you will become more keenly aware of the unpleasant and repugnant taste that such foods really have. As a result, this may be a turning point for you deciding to eat more natural and nutritious foods because the longer you chew these type foods, unexpected bursts of deep rich flavor are released. This is by Allah's design and Mercy. When taking time to eat at a slower pace and savor His foods with appreciation and gratitude, you will benefit from and be rewarded with an eating experience that will bring you much joy – and good health. *Which of the Favors of your Lord will you deny?*

Now is the time, too, before Ramadan, to pay attention to not *overeating*. Eating slower is a major component to not overeating; you will realize your point of satiation and fullness more easily. The stomach actually sends a chemical signal to the hypothalamus of the brain when it has had enough. When you eat too fast, you place food in your stomach so rapidly that the signal is not recognized by your brain until you have already consumed too much. There are even certain artificial substances in foods and drinks, (i.e. high fructose corn syrup), which will prevent the brain from being alerted when your stomach has reached its optimal capacity.

Make a conscious decision not to overeat. However, don't *rigidly* limit your eating, so you feel you're depriving yourself of healthy amounts of food. In fact, when foods are "grow foods" that come from the healthy soil of the earth, it is even desirable to eat many of them in abundance – such as green leafy vegetables. But still remember as the Prophet said and demonstrated in his own life, when you eat and drink you should strive to consume 1/3 food, and 1/3 drink with the remaining space in your stomach consisting of approximately 1/3 air.

Eating to the *point of energy*[12] is an excellent goal to set and work towards. In other words, eat to the point when you can sense your food beginning to boost the energy level in your body and you feel that your genuine body hunger has been appeased. It may take a little practice to make this discovery so learn to *listen* to your body **while you eat.** When you first sense you have had enough, stop! At least try; the more you attempt to do this, the easier it will get!

To prepare yourself for eating nutritiously during Ramadan, you must become acutely aware of the best energy producing foods you can get that are in season, within your budget and are accessible. Eating fruits and vegetables *in season* is very important. Allah actually created foods in each region of the earth with specific harvest times throughout the year to match varying physiological states in the body. For instance, after a long cold winter you are likely to have heavier congestion and dryness in your body due to artificial heating systems your body has been exposed to. This dry heat produces a condition called reactive mucous[13]. Your body then needs the lighter foods harvested in spring and summer in order to detox and cleanse from this mucous buildup.

Therefore, spring/summer foods are functional as well as lovely to eat. When you integrate them into your diet on a consistent basis you will feel light, airy, springy and more energetic. So start now to include fresh produce (lettuce, summer squash, melons, etc.) in your daily meals and you will be well on your way to creating sharper awareness and improved physical health, both which will accelerate your spiritual ascent during Ramadan.

This is a great time to start making green smoothies, fruit smoothies and combo smoothies a part of your breakfast routine. On page 163 is a **basic recipe for a green energy smoothie** that will start your body, from the inside out, vibrating with good health and feelings of energizing vitality!

In general, Ramadan is a good time to start shifting to lighter meals. Think simplicity. When you refrain from eating foods that require using complex ingredients and time-consuming methods of preparation, you are more closely aligned with how the Prophet (saw) ate. You may never reach the point where you can eat 3 dates for a complete meal and feel satisfied ☺, but perhaps, during Ramadan, you can realize that eating a few simple foods at a meal can be highly gratifying. A few recipes for simple, but nutritionally dense meals with plenty of taste and flavor start on page 162.

In preparation for Ramadan you may want to start doing trial fasts a few days per week (i.e., Monday's & Thursday's). The challenge of these practice fasts will be to focus not only on the fast itself, but breaking the fast using the information and suggestions that have been given in this section.

MAINTAIN Quality Eating During Ramadan

If you were able, before Ramadan, to take time to implement some of the recommendations made thus far and initiate a routine for using them, then you are well on your way to having a very good discipline for proper eating and diet during Ramadan. However, if you were unable to do so, then take time now to go over the first section and review the suggested concepts and principles of eating. Then, go forward in reading this section on how you can further build upon and use these principles during Ramadan.

Suhoor: Drink a full glass of water with a little lemon when you first get up. This will enhance the cleansing your body is experiencing through fasting. Then, jumpstart your daily Fast by including high quality protein, fruit and green veggies and a whole grain that will give you the nourishment and energy needed to sustain you through the hours of fasting.

You can get this nourishment from healthy foods found in the following categories:

> **Proteins** – small portions of (halal/tayyib)[14] meat, poultry, fish or beans; quinoa (a whole grain that is very high rich in protein – great for vegetarians). Oatmeal also has a hefty level of protein.
>
> **Fruits** – melons, apples, kiwis, oranges, and berries. Try to eat fruits in season and that are native to the region where you live.
>
> **Green veggies** – kale, spinach, broccoli, or chard
>
> **Whole grains** – 100% whole wheat, whole oats, steel oats, quinoa, brown rice, couscous, millet

There are many other healthy items that can be added to each of the food categories above, so feel free to explore and purchase high quality foods that have appeal to you and your family. The rule is to choose healthy, *quality* foods that nourish your body, not foods that deplete it of vital nutrients and energy.

As you get deeper into your Fast you will probably want less and less to eat, especially in the morning. However, it's best to get as much nutrient dense food in your body at suhoor as possible so your energy can be sustained and you won't become exhausted during the middle or towards the end of your fasting day. To accomplish this, I suggest that you drink a glass of green smoothie (pg. 163) along with a piece of whole grain toast and a good source of protein; egg, halal sausage, fish or tofu.

If that is still too much food, you can make a *super* green smoothie that is a **complete breakfast** by simply using the basic green smoothie recipe and adding protein powder (good suggestions include whey, hemp, or organic non-GMO soy) or raw whole oats. Peanut butter or other nut butters such as almond or cashew can also be added as a source of protein. Or adding a dollop of unsweetened yogurt can give you a healthy dose of protein. Combining a few of these "super foods" will give you the highest energetic charge available in a "one glass" meal. A few others you can add are chia seeds, goji berries or cacao beans.

Throughout your day take note of the times you feel the most energetic (or the opposite – tired or lethargic). Think back to what you ate for Suhoor or at Iftar the night before. Can you see a correlation between your state of body-mind and the foods you've been eating? Remember that what you eat is shaping and contributing to your daily reality. What you eat impacts your DNA on a cellular level; the foundation for building your body tissues, bones, organs and systems which in turn affect your emotions and intellectual faculties. Also your spirituality (the ability to feel an intimate connection with your Lord as well as to authentically interact with people and the natural creation) can be enhanced or limited relative to the foods you eat.

What you eat determines what your body looks and feels like physically, how you feel emotionally as well as how well your brain takes in and processes information. Therefore, if you feel cranky or irritable during the day or you find it difficult to remember things due to "brain fog", then seek to make an association between these feelings and the food you've consumed over the past 24 – 72 hours. Most of all listen to your body *very* carefully.

Many times just pausing a few seconds before you put food on your plate will give your body ample time to communicate to your mind what it wants or doesn't want and how much of it to eat. In fact, ask your body the question, *"what do you want?"* before choosing food and *expect* that it will give you a gentle prodding to steer you in the direction that is best. In this way you will constantly be uncovering new insights into which type foods give you the most energy and which ones to avoid.

Aggie Nashid, raw food chef in Atlanta Ga. states that, "Everything you eat should be a healing experience and benefit your body in some way. Even the snacks that you eat and the condiments you put on your food should be natural and healing. People should eat what likes them, not just what they like because of the taste. When you eat the food that likes you (i.e. food that is nutritious and aids the development of your body), then you will learn to love that food because it makes you feel so great." Also, she notes that, "when you stop eating dead, lifeless food (processed, junk, overcooked foods) you don't have to eat as much because live foods energize you and have you feeling wonderful!"[15]

Perhaps the hardest part of the Fast of Ramadan is to follow the prescribed commands given by Allah for breaking the Fast at Iftar. When you've been without food all day long, the natural tendency at first is to heartily attempt to make up for the meals you missed. The only way to truly offset this inclination, particularly when you're first adapting to the fasting regimen, is to remember that Allah through His Prophet has made eating a simple meal (i.e. the meal of a poor man) a critical injunction of the Fast.

I believe this command is not only to humble and sensitize us to those who have little to eat, but to keep us from committing the major error of overeating. Why? Because overeating impairs digestion – food that is not broken down properly literally sits and rots in the digestive system, setting up new sources of toxins that limit our body's ability to rid itself of these additional poisons. Toxins can make you feel sluggish and lazy while fasting and set up sites for inflammation and infection throughout your body.

Again, when you learn to *listen* to your body it will be much easier not to overeat when you break your Fast. Your body will tell you when it's full if you just listen. Here are some helpful tips in maintaining the limits when eating Iftar.

- Seek to connect with the purpose for eating the food you're about to consume. Hopefully, it is quality food that you have mindfully chosen and are aware of its benefit to you. You're not just eating to satisfy your immediate hunger, nor your taste buds, but because the food you have chosen possesses nutritive value and energy your body needs.

- Here are some practical things to do when faced with an escalating appetite that worsens with a huge array of foods displayed before you (which may occur when breaking Fast at the masjid or in someone's home):
    - **Immediately break your Fast by drinking a full glass of water** and then eat a few dates. Dates are excellent for breaking the Fast because they help with digestion and with curbing your appetite. However, I would not suggest eating more than three (the

sunnah tradition). Dried fruits such as dates contain high amounts of sugar; if you eat many of them at one time, your blood sugar will spike and you may later experience overwhelming tiredness or sleepiness. Not good, if you plan to make Tarawih salat or need to catch up on reading the Qur'an. Plus, continual elevation in blood sugar levels can lead to *insulin resistance*[16], a precursor to diabetes and other chronic serious illnesses.

o **Drink another full glass of water after Maghrib Salat.** Your body may still be in need of extra hydration – and remember sometimes hunger is mistaken for thirst. That ravenous appetite you have may primarily be due to your body's need for more water.

o **Make a spontaneous and heartfelt du'a before you eat.** Express gratitude for the chain of events and people that led to the food being in front of you. Be thankful for the benefit that the food will give, seek Allah's protection from any unseen harm in the food and His help from eating too much.

o **Chew well and pause after each mouthful.** That way you will realize when you have had enough. Your stomach will signal your brain when to stop. If you eat too quickly, you will shove food into your stomach before your brain picks up the signal. Stop eating before you get any tightness in your stomach indicating you are full to the brim with food. Remember 1/3 drink, 1/3 food, 1/3 air!

When eating at home you have greater control over the quantity of food that is prepared for your Iftar. If you don't fix large amounts of food, then it's pretty effortless not to overeat, right? ☺ When standing in front of the refrigerator trying to decide what you're going to cook for Iftar, keep reminding yourself of the Prophet's (SAW) main dietary rule - simplicity, simplicity, simplicity! However, when relating to aggressive human drives like hunger and appetite, this advice is most assuredly easier said than done.

First, there's the difficult hurdle of *habit* to overcome (you and your family being accustomed to large, varied amounts of food for dinner). The second major challenge that can surface during Ramadan is a phenomenon I refer to as *"food fantasies."* A food fantasy is prone to occur mid-morning or sometime late in the afternoon when your mind is anticipating what it normally would eat for a noon or evening meal. When your fasting brain then realizes it won't be eating lunch at all and that dinner is going to be significantly delayed, a flood of food fantasies can arise.

This is the time you may start *thinking or obsessing* about eating your favorite cheese cake and topping it off with gourmet coffee, gorging on your favorite meal of macaroni and cheese, fried chicken and collard greens, or falafel, lamb and samosa, or reaching in the glove compartment of your car for your private stash of candy and chips.

In addition, if you are the main cook in the house, *food fantasies* may escalate into hours of looking through colorful magazines or internet recipes for new, interesting and often times elaborate ways to prepare a blowout Iftar meal for your family and guests. Also, individual food fantasies can sometimes balloon into *food fantasy collectives* where several people are drawn into extended conversations about the delicious, appetizing, mouth-watering foods they would love to have for the coming night's Iftar.

Is there anything wrong with these "little" self-indulgent daydreams about food? After all, you're still fasting; you're not actually eating the food, right? Initially your body may really be in some form of "shock" from not eating when it is accustomed, so a few illusions or delusions about food can be expected. I'm not actually suggesting that indulging in food fantasies invalidates your Fast; however spending time thinking extensively about food during your day of fasting is probably not the most productive way to receive its benefits. Remember, through the fasting experience, you want to reach your highest and most empowered self possible – physically, mentally, emotionally and spiritually – and to receive your greatest reward from your Lord (SWT)!

To offset these imaginative indulgences that can be mentally and spiritually draining as well as distracting I suggest pre-planning your daily Ramadan meals. Using a menu plan throughout the month can go a long way in making the preparation, cooking and dining experience of meals much simpler and more consistent so that an inordinate amount of time is not spent thinking (i.e. fantasizing) of what to cook for you and your family. A sample menu planning template is available on pg. 178 and downloadable at **www.footstepstowellness.net**.

Here are tips on how to use it:

- **Set aside a designated time to create a list of healthy food items** that fit the criteria discussed in this section thus far – foods that are simple, nutritious, easy to prepare and appetizing. Use the meal planning template to write down what you will have each day for Iftar and Suhoor.

- **Meal planning will eliminate the need to come up with ideas for meal preparation while you are fasting – which are likely to trigger food fantasies.** Meal planning will give you the assurance of knowing, at a glance, what your meals will be for the day and also ensure the needed items are on hand so you don't need to run to the store at the last minute to purchase something.

- **Most importantly, creating a menu plan will free up brain space so that you can devote your mental and spiritual energies to furthering your self-development** by engaging in other more relevant areas of the Fast such as studying Qur'an, doing supererogatory prayers, performing acts of charity, etc. and challenging yourself with brain and soul enhancing activities that are stimulating and fulfilling. See Chapter 11.

SUSTAIN Quality Eating After Ramadan

If you went on a food binge during Eid celebrations, it's still easy for a while after that to continue eating smaller amounts of food since your stomach is greatly reduced in size from processing less food for 29 to 30 days. And, if you have been successful in absorbing much of the information in this manual and following its guidelines, then you are on your way to establishing an improved dietary style that will carry you well beyond this Ramadan into the months preceding the next one.

However, due to intense media and social environments thrusting food at us from every direction via TV commercials, magazine and internet ads, billboards, phone apps, an increasing arena of restaurants in every neighborhood as well as gluttonous amounts of tantalizing foods stocked on the grocery shelves, gradually appetites based on artificially stimulated desires increase and once again you may find that you're not eating the best type-foods nor eating them in the best manner. Once again you may revert to mindlessly eating without giving thoughtful consideration to the impact that food choices and habits are having on your body. Additionally, stress from the daily challenges of living may creep in and adversely compound this situation.

However, taking time out to relax, center yourself, breathe deeply and reflect deeply on the lessons and disciplines that have been gained during Ramadan can turn things around. After all, you victoriously just went through the most challenging and most enlightening period of the year and you proved, without doubt, that you have the self-restraint and discipline needed to do whatever you desire with sincere motivation, faith and trust in Allah! You focused on pleasing your Lord by not eating or drinking during most of your waking hours; now you can continue to focus on pleasing Him by restraining from exceeding the limits of what is healthy and beneficial for your body, mind and soul. Insha'Allah, you have developed an enhanced vision for attaining, with Allah's

Help, a higher level of consciousness for functioning in your role as khalifah and being empowered to better serve Him and His creation.

Though dietary choices are probably one of the most difficult life habits in which to cultivate positive change, it can be done. You've just spent substantial time during Ramadan devoted to a more enhanced way of life that included an elevated dietary style; so know that with strong intentions, commitment, focus, proactive action and determination you can continue. Here is a summary and additional tips for sustaining and improving the nutritional intake of quality foods for you and your family until the next Ramadan:

- **Listen to your body.** Know the difference between real hunger and a desire to eat for other reasons such as comfort, boredom or emotional stress.

- **Don't make eating a form of entertainment.** Identify other things that give you joy and engage your energy so that you don't live to eat, but that you eat to live! See Chapter 11 for more information on this topic.

- **Eat the highest quality food that your budget will allow.** Continue to eat simple foods rather than rich, elaborate food combinations. Eat mostly plant based foods – vegetables, fruits and grains – with meat and chicken eaten in smaller amounts. Eat more fish and seafood that is fresh and caught in the wild (not raised on fish farms). Sumayya Allen, urban agriculturist with Truly Living Farms in Atlanta Ga., cautions to not just look for organic foods, but seek to purchase foods that are natural, fresh and local. Getting food from a garden or farm to your plate as soon as possible is very important and best for your health. Nutrients in the food will be greatly diminished if the foods come from a long distance away." Sumayya suggests going to **www.localharvest.org** to search for farms, farmers' markets and organic growers in your area to make purchases of fresh foods.[17]

- **If snacking between meals, eat healthy snacks** that are mainly protein-based (not laden with salt, sugars, refined flours and artificial ingredients).

- **Limit your intake of processed foods** and do more home cooking using natural whole foods rather than boxed convenience foods or eating out at restaurants.

- **Use the 90/10 or at least the 80/20 rule for eating.** This means to consciously eat the best healthy foods you can 80 – 90% of the time and the remaining 10 – 20% of the time eat whatever you want. Increasingly, the "whatever you want" phase will consist of healthier food choices; at some point your body won't allow you to continue eating what's bad for it without immediate repercussions. Gradually, your taste buds will become trained to want only pleasure from eating truly quality foods.

- **Connect with the good feelings that having good health produces.** Seek to stay on a level of possessing high energy, vitality and having good mental and spiritual clarity and focus. When you don't feel this way look at the food you're eating; it's creating you on all levels. Continue keeping a journal from time to time so you can connect what you're eating with how you feel and thereby help you identify the foods that make you feel good as opposed to the foods that make you feel poorly.

- **Hire a health coach if you're having problems doing it alone.** Many individuals who want to excel in their fields find coaches to help them reach their best level of performance. Striving to achieve higher levels in dietary health and healthy lifestyle practices should be no different. Holistic health coaching can help you better connect with the voice within that is giving guidance towards the things you need to embrace in order to achieve the optimal health you are seeking. Due to emotional and stagnant habits and beliefs you may be experiencing extreme difficulty in the struggle to reach your goals.

A health coach who is holistically trained can aid you in developing strategies to become more proactive in staying on the path to reach heights you are longing to achieve within your body, mind and soul! Go to **www.footstepstowellness.net** for more information.

Reflection:

1. What are you learning when you listen to your body? What does it want? What doesn't it want?

2. What new foods are you committed to including in your diet and which ones will you stay away from?

3. What obstacles keep popping up that are preventing you from improving your diet in order to obtain a healthy body?

4. What will you commit to do in order to overcome these obstacles to achieve your dietary goals?

Section 2

Nourish Your Life with More than Food

What contributes to the sustenance of your life are not just the foods on your plate or the drinks you place in your mouth, but *whatever* you do, think and feel – in fact, *everything* you experience in life is being absorbed and metabolized by your body-mind-soul system. Therefore, feeling good about the work you do, engaging in activities you enjoy, having loving relationships with family and friends, enjoying the stimulation of learning something new, and even getting a good night's sleep are all things that offer nourishment in the same way your body gets sustenance and fulfillment from physical food.

The next set of chapters address these other "food" sources and provide critical information about additional holistic health practices which can determine your capacity to achieve and maintain healthy levels of energy and vibrancy during and after Ramadan.

Chapter 9 – Exercise Means Movement

Allah knows how you move about and how you dwell
in your homes. . . .
Al-Qur'an 47:19

As a human being with the unique gift of free will, you are created to move with a *conscious* sense of direction and purpose! Allah has given you 600+ muscle attachments that interface with your skeletal system to allow you to execute tens of thousands of actions throughout your day. Though most of these movements are minute and occur involuntarily, many others are produced through *intentional thought* and *consciousness* that can lead to greater productivity and achievement. Therefore, strengthening and conditioning your body to optimally function and perform increases its capacity to carry out the numerous demands made by your intellect and soul. This is a key component in the formula for moving towards success in your role as khalifah! [See Chapter 4.]

Since your body is built for powerful action, it is imperative that you give it not only quality nutrition, water and breath for building quality performance, but that you also condition it at regular intervals with rigorous movement – i.e. exercise. For some people though, exercise is a dreaded activity which they hardly ever do, while others workout vigorously believing it is a "magic bullet" that will automatically erase the effects of a bad diet. In the first group are people who represent the classic "couch potatoes" – their workouts consist of moving their fingers up and down on the TV remote or going back and forth to the refrigerator during commercial breaks. In the second group are those who often make a mad dash to the gym after chronic overeating or binging on junk food to try to undo the negative effect the consumption of such foods invariably will have on their bodies.

Between these two extremes are a growing number of people who realize that great nutrition and great exercise *must* go hand in hand in order to have really great health. Why? The purpose of exercise is not only to burn calories to keep your body fit and trim and keep your weight down, but to also more powerfully utilize the food (i.e. fuel) that you give it. This is the metabolic process at work and usually the higher your metabolic rate, the more efficiently your food/fuel is burned and the more energy is produced to optimize the functioning of your body's systems.

Exercise not only raises metabolism to increase energy, it also provides a plethora of other benefits such as detoxification, blood purification, stress relief and many other health rewards, including weight loss and fat reduction. Working out also improves mood and reduces tension because with regular exercise, critical brain chemicals like serotonin and dopamine are raised – the very same ones synthetically produced as active ingredients in prescription drugs for treatment of depression and anxiety disorders. Yet, despite the fact that essential connections between consistent exercise and quality health are easily made, it still is quite difficult for many people to get into the exercise habit.

For those who do little to no exercise, stretching is great preparation for beginning any exercise program. In fact, because stretching is such a simple exercise which increases flexibility and improves range of motion, Ramadan is an ideal time to develop a habit of *daily* stretching. Quite easy to do if you are starting to really listen to your body because stretching is something it naturally inclines to, particularly after a full night's sleep. When first getting out of bed or rising up from jalsa after doing your fajr salat, simply stand up and stretch for a few minutes in any direction your body feels the need to go. To get a really good, elongated stretch hold the position for a few seconds before moving to another, but don't bounce as you can strain your muscles or tendons. Stretching should really be done when changing from any sedentary position – whether after sleeping, resting or sitting at a computer for several hours on end.

If you're just getting into or back into an exercise regimen and want to start off slowly with stretching as your main focus for exercise during Ramadan, it would be good to also add a few low impact aerobic moves or a short walking routine. Aerobic exercise is to perform at a level which increases your breathing and heart rate, thus assuring that your metabolism has been raised. This is not only important for increasing your energy and improving digestion, but also for enhancing the cleansing process while fasting.

Exercise forms such as yoga, tai chi or qigong are also excellent to engage in while fasting because they use a combination of stretching, deep breathing, and inner visualization to gently condition the body while at the same time aiding in the enhancement of body-mind-soul purification. Qigong, considered "moving meditation" integrates body, mind and breath as you go through a series of flowing movements. Tai chi and many yoga forms (i.e. Vinyasa, Kundalini) offer similar benefits and can be safely practiced by just about anyone even while fasting. Always though, listen to your body and if you get any indication that you are overexerting yourself, particularly while fasting, then stop immediately.

For those of you accustomed to intense aerobic, cardiovascular, weight lifting or high impact sports use your personal discernment as a gauge as to what degree to continue during Ramadan. You may not want to stop entirely, nor is that necessarily recommended, but because of your body's response to the process of fasting or because of a high heat period of fasting, you may want to cut back to a moderate workout. Any type of rigorous activity during the hours of fasting should be discouraged completely, if possible.

Always seek to be well-hydrated and have a light meal under your belt before engaging in a full exercise routine and be mindful of not exercising on a full stomach. That means the ideal time for exercise is about an hour after Iftar and at least 30 minutes before Suhoor. However, be aware that vigorous exercise can very well delay your ability to fall asleep later. If you are getting up early in the morning to exercise, then make sure you drink plenty of water plus perhaps consume a light healthy drink like green tea or fresh raw juice. After you've finished your workout, you can eat your Suhoor meal.

Haneefah Salim, personal fitness trainer out of Baltimore, Maryland, cautions avid exercisers not to let their desire to squeeze in a workout detract from the obligations and rituals of the Fast. Especially, "do not seek to replace prayer with exercise." In other words, if it comes down to whether to work out after Iftar or make 'Isha and Tarawih, then choose the obvious – what is most pleasing to your Lord. Very wisely Haneefah adds, "Completing all the obligatory prayers and the extra prayers is an exercise in itself."[18]

After Ramadan, seek to cultivate exercise as a regular part of your life. If the "e" word still repels you and you dread the idea of consistently working out because you fear it will be too overwhelming, boring or time consuming, know that exercise doesn't have to be limited to going to a gym, working out with a DVD, running on a treadmill in your home or running around a track at the local high school. When you see exercise simply as moving in a directed and dedicated fun way that pushes your body to vigorously perform, then a whole range of possibilities opens up -- biking, skating, tennis, hiking, dancing, swimming, or playing tag or hide-and-go-seek with your children. If it's hard to consider where to begin, try to remember the types of activities you enjoyed as a child; activities where you got hot, sweaty and a healthy "worn out" feeling at the end – and you had loads of fun doing it!

If you think of exercise as doing movements you really love, then many times boring routines and tedious postures can take a back seat. However, the consistency and repetition of a structured exercise program can also prove very beneficial. After all, it is the recurring cycles and organized systems in creation that allow life to have order and to productively grow.

According to Haneefah, an average weekly workout best consists of cardio (aerobic) exercise, strength/resistance training (i.e. lunges, weights, push-ups) and exercises such as yoga or Pilates that tone your core area – your mid-section to your hip bone. She states that resistance exercises are particularly needed as people age because after 40 (for women) and 60 (for men), there's an average 8% reduction of muscle mass every ten years. Yet, with focused commitment and support from a personal trainer, this muscle loss oftentimes can be regained and strengthened within about three months.

Even though 30 – 45 minutes daily, four to five times a week, is the suggested time allotment to receive the full benefit of regular exercise, your workouts can be divided into shorter periods throughout the day. For example, for a daily total of 30 minutes of exercise you can do two 15 minutes workouts or even three 10 minute workouts. You might want to engage in 15 minutes of yoga in the morning and then a balance of cardio exercises, strength training and/or vigorous fun activities later in the day. However, Haneefah advises that a sizeable portion of your overall exercise routine should be spent exerting yourself within 60 – 85% of your maximum heart rate. This will give you a high energy workout and put you in a zone where you are burning fat.

To calculate your targeted heart rate, start with the number 200 and subtract your age. That number represents your **maximum** heart rate; next calculate 65% of this number and then 85% of it to get your full *targeted heart rate range* during your workout.

Example: 200 – 40 (your age) = 160 (your maximum heart rate). 65% of 160 = 96. 85% of 160 = 136. Therefore, your targeted heart rate during active exercise or activity is in the range of 96 to 136 beats per minute. You can best determine whether you are reaching this range by pausing your activity, taking your pulse for 10 seconds, and then multiplying by 6 to find out your heart rate for one full minute.[19]

It is important to watch out for light-headedness, nausea, headaches and muscle cramping during your workout. If you experience any of these symptoms while exercising, stop or at least slow down because this may indicate you have a medical condition that needs to be addressed. Remember, particularly if you are just beginning to develop an exercise routine, it is highly recommended that you check with your doctor before engaging in any vigorous program or activity.

In summary, what's the best way to start an exercise program and keep it up? The main thing is to do *some*thing; keep it moving! If you can't do a lot because of your daily schedule or your physical condition, then do what you can. Having a fit, functioning, flexible, fluid body is needed to provide the foundation for the holistically-based health you are seeking. Choose some type of exercise you feel you can commit to and get going!

Reflection:

1. What are the main obstacles that stop you from exercising?

2. What can you do differently to move these obstacles out of your way?

3. What fun, vigorous activity can you start doing so you enjoy exercising?

4. What type of exercise will you do during Ramadan? When will you do it?

5. What is an exercise routine you can keep up after Ramadan that excites you and makes you want to keep it moving?

<u>Chapter 10 – Your Body's Right to Rest and Sleep</u>

He it is that has made the Night that you might rest therein and
the Day to make things visible to you . . .
Holy Qur'an 10:67

Everything in creation alternates between movement and rest that
are similar to the cycle of the alternation of night and day. Rest
(which includes sleep, a deeper component of rest), is a necessary
balance to movement and is essential for relaxation, rejuvenation of
energy and even reorientation for direction. The Prophet (saw)
made this universal principle clear simply by stating that your body
has rights over you. That means Allah has given your physical
body permission to make demands on you (i.e. your soul) for its
requirements – and rest/sleep is a primary need your body has that
must be fulfilled in *sufficient* amounts.

Do you know about 1/3 of your total existence is spent in the world
of sleep? When sleep, you lose consciousness, your physical body is

on auto-pilot and you enter another reality where Allah says that your soul is returned to Him, each and every night. While your soul is in the realm of the Divine Presence of your Creator some amazing things are taking place inside your physical body. Your biological systems which have been taxed during their daily performance are being replenished and restored; your cells, tissues and organs are literally being swept of microscopic debris, and being rebuilt and repaired where needed. Even the information your brain took in over the course of the day is being filed, sorted and stored for long term memory. What goes on in your sleep is similar to what happens in a 24-hour store at night after the heavy traffic of the day has died down and you see workers sweeping, cleaning, restocking and putting things back in place.

Therefore, depriving yourself of the full benefits of your body's important transition from movement to deep rest is not a good idea. Bertram Brooks, sleep lab technologist, says that, "People pay a price when they give up sleep time. Every time you don't get the proper amount of sleep that you need, your body goes into a deficit – a sleep debt. The more sleep debt that you acquire, the more apt you are to be less productive and less attentive during your waking hours. This can impair your ability to think clearly, make sound judgments and the adeptness of your natural reflexes. Many automobile and work accidents occur when people lapse into periods of micro-sleep (10 – 15 seconds) because of sleep deprivation. Also, experiencing chronic sleep deprivation can lead to a serious reduction in immune system function resulting in more colds, illnesses; even a susceptibility to serious dis-eases like diabetes and cancer."[20]

During every waking hour of the Fast of Ramadan there are innumerable rewards bestowed upon the fasting believers for their remembrance of Allah, their performance of the ritualistic practices and their engagement in meritorious acts. Consequently, some Muslims believe that sleep throughout the month should be minimized. However, the Prophet (saw) in his famous Ramadan Sermon stated that during the Blessed Month even "sleep is worship". So don't think you must push your body beyond its need for proper rest at this time to be in Allah's Favor. Again, restful sleep is needed for systemic repair and rejuvenation and a body not receiving adequate amounts of this bounty can undergo deprivation that can impact its overall health.

Yet, as you get deeper into the Fast, you will probably experience increasing levels of alertness to the extent that you feel you don't need as much sleep as usual. As your body requires less and less energy for digestion and other processes related to the regular consumption of food, your mental and spiritual faculties become more fully awake. In fact, in many other religions, cultures and health circles, dietary fasting is practiced solely so that this spiritual awakening can occur. However, no other fasting practice, not even the Sunnah fasts the Prophet (saw) engaged in throughout the year, can match the bounteous depth, beauty and blessings that are promised during the Fast of Ramadan! This includes the unparalleled special, intimate closeness you develop with your Lord during this time!

So you don't want to miss the opportunity to experience the spiritual highs that can be achieved only by being in a consciously aware state during the hours of fasting. You certainly don't want to sleep for long periods while fasting and then stay up during the night so you can eat and engage in frivolous activities. It is wise to get as much sleep as possible after your nightly prayers. This is not easy to accomplish during the summer months when 'Isha Salat comes in late followed by the performance of many rak'ats of Tarawih, only to wake up a few hours later for Suhoor. Yet, you must seek, somehow, to squeeze in your required sleep and rest. Perhaps you can go back to bed for a while after Fajr or carve time out during the day for a brief siesta.

When you really just can't sleep the hours your body requires, then try to lie down or sit very still for a while so your body can rest; this can offer significant benefits as well. Deep breathing while resting can further rejuvenate the body and even benefit your overall health in much the same way as full sleep. Plus, after a few rounds of deep breathing, you are likely to fall asleep if you had difficulty in doing so before.

After Ramadan's somewhat eclectic schedule that sometimes produces irregular sleep, it's important to settle into a regular nightly regimen to consistently give your body its due. Though it's usually recommended that an adult get 7 – 9 hours of sleep every night, learn your bio-individual requirement by determining how much you need not to feel tired or lethargic the next day.

Don't fall into the increasing category of people who are sleeping less so they can have a longer day to work and spend leisure hours. That is not wise. As a result, you may often find yourself depending on stimulants (i.e. caffeine, "energy" supplements) to falsely charge your body with energy and wonder why you have difficulty falling asleep later. After a while you may end up with chronic insomnia and have to take something to induce sleep every night because your body's natural sleep/wake cycle has been disrupted.

If you are having problems with insomnia or simply don't feel completely refreshed or rejuvenated when you get up in the morning, here are some recommendations for helping you get a deep and more restful sleep throughout the night[21]:

1. **Decide to go to bed at the same time each night** (as early as possible) and get up at the same time each morning. The body best responds to cycles that occur at set times. Your body (particularly your adrenal system) does the majority of its recharging between the hours of 11 p.m. and 1 a.m. In addition, your gallbladder dumps toxins during this same period. If you are awake, the toxins back up into your liver, which can harm your health.

2. **Create an environment in your bedroom that encourages relaxation and sleep.** Don't have a TV, computer or electronic equipment in your bedroom. You don't want to have anything that will distract you from the main focus of getting in bed and relaxing until you naturally fall asleep.

3. **At least 30 minutes to an hour before your bedtime, start to wind down.** Don't have your mind active with work or intense activities up until the time you get in bed. You need to go to sleep feeling calm, not hyped or anxious about what may take place the next day.

4. **Don't drink any fluids within 2 hours of going to bed.** This will reduce the likelihood of needing to go to the bathroom, or at least minimize the frequency.

5. **Avoid before-bed snacks, particularly bread, baked goods and sugars.** These will raise your blood sugar and delay sleep. Later, when blood sugar drops too low, you may wake up and be unable to fall back asleep. Eat a high-protein snack *several hours* **before** going to bed. This can provide a good source of L-tryptophan, an important amino acid needed for melatonin and serotonin production, which help to induce relaxation and sleep.

6. **Read something spiritual or uplifting.** This may help you relax. Don't read anything stimulating, such as a mystery or suspense novel, which has the opposite effect. In addition, if you are really enjoying a suspenseful book, you might be tempted to continue reading for hours, instead of going to sleep!

7. **Establish a bedtime routine.** This could include meditation, deep breathing, using aromatherapy or essential oils or indulging in a massage from your mate. The key is to find something that is relaxing, then repeat it each night to help you release the tensions of the day.

8. **Make certain you are exercising regularly.** Exercising for at least 30 minutes per day can improve your sleep. However, don't exercise too close to bedtime; it may keep you awake.

9. **Listen to relaxation CDs.** Some people find the sound of white noise or nature, such as the ocean or forest, to be soothing for sleep.

10. **Block out all light.** Even a night light, light from an alarm clock or moonlight streaming in through your window can interfere with your body's circadian rhythm. This will disrupt its ability to totally relax and stay asleep. It is very important to sleep in as close to complete darkness as possible.

11. **Lose excess weight.** Being overweight can increase your risk of sleep apnea and other sleep disorders, which can seriously impair your sleep and endanger your health.

12. **Stay well-hydrated during the day and avoid caffeine.** Even an afternoon cup of caffeinated coffee or tea will keep some people from falling asleep at night. Be aware that some sodas and medications also contain caffeine.

Give your body the sleep it needs on a regular basis. Remember prolonged sleep deprivation can compromise your immune system, causing you to be susceptible to a variety of infections and illnesses, even cancers. Your body has rights over you! Eating nutritious energizing foods coupled with consistent adequate rest and sleep will give your body the correct balance to move forward with vigor and vitality to facilitate the changes leading to your further development and personal transformation!

<u>Reflection:</u>

1. How much sleep do you need on a regular basis to feel your best?

2. Do you have any difficulties falling asleep and staying asleep for the full night? If so, pinpoint what your issues are and use one or more of the tips listed above to address them.

NOTE: If you are experiencing any serious sleep issues like apnea or even prolonged snoring (which can be an indication of apnea) make an appointment to see your doctor. You may be referred to a sleep specialist or a sleep clinic for further study of your problem.

Chapter 11 - Re-create and Nourish Your Intellect

"We endowed them with faculties of hearing, seeing,
heart and intellect . . ."
Holy Qur'an 46:26

The beauty and uniqueness of Ramadan is that it is a complete Fast – not only mandating that your body become engaged in the rigors of physical fasting, but also requiring that you work on elevating your mental, spiritual and social development through prayer, the study of the Holy Qur'an and positive, wholesome communal exchange.

This prescription works fine when sticking closely to the rituals associated with the Fast by reading a thirtieth of the Holy Qur'an every day, performing the obligatory and supererogatory Salat, and interacting with other fasting believers during community and social iftars. However, in the hours during the day and evening when not doing things directly related to the basic injunctions of the Fast, you may often end up occupying your mind with activities that are counterproductive to the personal growth you are seeking at this most bountiful time.

In order to truly profit from the opportunities available to your awakened mind, which is blossoming as your body continues to abstain from physical sustenance during the daylight hours, you need to engage in stimulating and thought-provoking activities. The mind and the body, during Ramadan, need to continually be involved in things that are revitalizing their energies and propelling them to higher and higher levels. During Ramadan, enjoyment should consist of *re-creational* activities (acts that replenish and rejuvenate your creative energy), not mindless forms of entertainment that "dumb down" your intellect by catering to your baser desires.

Is it logical to abstain from food, which is a lawful bodily desire, only to occupy your mind with things unlawful? Movies, TV programming and books promoting immoral or unethical behaviors, frivolities, vanities and addictions are not intelligent pastimes during Ramadan. Ramadan should not only free you from food and drink (during the fasting hours), but all things not supportive of your body-mind-soul development at any time throughout the month.

That doesn't mean to not enjoy Ramadan and sometimes have just plain (halal) fun! Actually healthy enjoyment is easy to achieve simply by being involved in things that naturally align with your beautiful human nature. First seek enjoyment and pleasure in the lawful things Allah has commanded during the Fast. Avoid being on "automatic" while performing the ritualistic practices of the Fast; *take time* to enjoy their intrinsic value – *sloowly* make salat, savoring the special communication with your Creator, *sloowly* recite and read the Holy Qur'an – reflecting on its subtleties and nuances, and *sloowly* ponder the many facets of Allah's creation including the magnificence of your own unique self.

Take nature walks; go to the library to get books, DVD's or audio tapes on interesting topics that will educate you and your family; listen to music of various cultures; create new hobbies or projects with family members and friends. Get involved in all types of charitable acts, not only feeding the hungry, which is admirable, but doing other things that will benefit those who are in need. Have elevated conversations regarding ideas and concepts you're learning. Turn the TV off and think, act and do; not just you, but your whole family!

Also, take time each day to give thought to your life's vision and keep a running list of creative thoughts and ideas that come to you for working towards its success. You may not have the time or energy to fully execute a plan for carrying out the necessary steps to realize your vision, but you can contemplate the steps you will need to actively take once Ramadan ends. Get a notebook for recording the inspirations that will surely come to you when you experience moments of spiritual stillness – when you are more finely attuned and your creativity is flowing.

A wonderful activity for you or for your family to engage in before Ramadan is to brainstorm a list of halal, stimulating and enjoyable activities that can be done together or alone during the Month – and after. You can decide on activities that can be done weekly and plug them into the Activity Planning Template on pg. 179. This way, just as with the benefit of planning meals, creating a menu of weekly activities will eliminate the stress of coming up with something suitable to do "in the moment." It is then, when you will most likely default to the usual "fun" fare of watching TV, playing video games, surfing the internet or talking aimlessly on the phone.

Here's a list that my husband and I brainstormed together:

1. Visit one shut-in person every week and take flowers or some healthy goodies.
2. Go to the library and check out a few videos on something we've wanted to learn about – i.e. crocheting (me), playing guitar (him)
3. Drive to the nearest high point in our area to watch the sunrise after making Fajr.
4. Grab some water colors and paint a colorful abstract that expresses our love for the Deen.
5. Pull out the Scrabble board and make up a new rule – if we spell words related to Ramadan or that are English spellings of Arabic words we get bonus points.
6. Look up ayats related to nature in the Qur'an and take a walk in the park or sit under a tree to reflect on their meaning.
7. Go online to **www.lumosity.com** and play fun "brain" games that help with learning flexibility, speed, memory, problem-solving and more. [Note: To have full access to the

site you have to pay a subscription fee, but you can get a trial and enjoy some of the games free of charge.]

8. Bookmark film documentaries from **www.documentaryheaven.com** or **www.topdocumentaryfilms.com** in varied categories. Place these in a folder marked "edutainment" that we can view when we have time.

9. Make 10 or more bagged sandwiches and take to downtown areas to pass out to homeless individuals that we see on the streets.

10. Call extended family members (that we haven't talked to in a *loong* time) to learn how they're doing and share information with them about Ramadan.

Now, get your own creative juices flowing. There's space at the end of this chapter where you can begin brainstorming your list. Use the Activity Planning template on page 179 in the event that you feel susceptible to being drawn into the TV or internet doldrums or going to sleep in order to pass the time until Iftar. Making your list visibly accessible will allow you and your family to immediately view mentally stimulating and soul satisfying alternatives.

Hopefully, after an invigorating month of operating on an enhanced level of intellectual and creative proficiency, you will continue to be involved in these type activities as opposed to the ordinary, mundane and sometimes profane. Strive to occupy your time with an increased appetite for an array of worthy activities. Satisfying the intellect and the soul are key elements for *feeling* and *being* healthy and whole.

<u>Exercise:</u>

1. Brainstorm a list of nourishing and stimulating activities you (and your family) can do instead of watching TV or being on the internet.

Chapter 12 - Work with Purpose and Fulfillment

To each among you have We prescribed a law and a defined way . . .
Holy Qur'an 5:48

The work that you do each day should, in some way, be intellectually and spiritually gratifying, not just a series of thankless, boring tasks performed for pay. Yet, many people hate their jobs which results in yet another source of stress that can lead to sickness and dis-ease. Doing work that you love, are passionate about and that provides a needed service, resource or skill which contributes to others is not only rewarding in a feel good sort of way, but is most beneficial to your health.

Even if this type work doesn't represent your primary source of income, at least try, on a consistent basis, to engage in *something* you feel benefits others and nourishes your soul in some way. This may be through a hobby, volunteer work or just fulfilling neighborly needs.

Hopefully you can receive an income for doing work that you love. Being on a job that you hate, with people you don't like and who don't support, respect and value your true worth can be an energy-drainer and definitely will lead to various forms of illness.

> The American Psychology Association states that: Constant preoccupation with job responsibilities often leads to erratic eating habits and not enough exercise, resulting in weight problems, high blood pressure, and elevated cholesterol levels. Also, if you work in a hostile job environment and/or work long hours with pay that doesn't do justice to your perceived true worth, then you are more likely a candidate for heart disease, heart attacks and depression or mental burnout.[22]

Strive to develop your skills and education for getting the type of job that can make you happy. Better yet, strive to develop your passion and hobbies into a business endeavor that can sustain your family and contribute to others. Both of these strategies can make a huge difference, not just in the possibility of increasing your income, but in elevating your disposition, mood and energy levels, thereby greatly contributing to your quest for optimal health and living.

The idea of turning what you love doing into a source of income may seem scary and overwhelming at first. It may seem too self-indulgent or self-centered to pursue a job or develop a business where you are busy doing what you actually enjoy – for pay. The average worker associates their job with "necessary" drudgery and has accepted to be on daily autopilot for the rest of their productive years to get a paycheck. One's life is sacrificed in this way to pay bills, get the basic necessities of life and as many gratifying material goods as possible in order to experience "the good life". Many individuals are doing this not just for themselves, but for the love and care of their families.

But, does it have to be like this? Certainly Allah has given a prescribed purpose and path to each of His human creatures for serving Him and contributing to their fellow beings. It is those individuals that seek to know and understand the unique offerings of their souls who are given the insight and tools to develop their special gifts for offerings in the marketplace so that significant contributions can be made to their families, their communities and society. Once again, what better time to reflect and ponder on all of these possibilities than during the Blessed Month of Ramadan? You've already created a vision for full expression of your life that is pleasing to your Lord; why not also petition Him to guide you to what you must do to turn your vision into a viable livelihood?

Yes, petition Him and record the impressions and insights He blesses your soul to receive during this special Month! Be diligent in exploring the practical steps you need to take to make your vision an income-producing reality. This will be a process that more than likely will unfold over time rather than happening overnight. So you may need to remain in your less-than-optimal job right now; but you are in the process of developing a very bright and tangible future that should keep you energized and stimulated each day as you work towards realizing your vision.

Don't forget, too, that it is an obligation for the Muslim community to expansively grow in order to meet the needs of its members through the development of lawful (halal) businesses. There is a hadith which states that Allah will judge each community of Muslims regarding whether they fulfilled their communal obligation and the whole community will be punished for any need that has not been met. However, if any one individual moves forward to meet a need in the community, then the whole community is absolved and is rewarded. How wonderful to know that when you step into your unique purpose in offering needed products and services to other believers, that not only are you helping them, yourself and your family, but you are also aiding the soul of your community in this life and the next!

Reflection:

1. What is it that you love doing that engages your intellect and skills and is of benefit to others?

2. Review your vision and think about aspects of it could be turned into some type of income producing endeavor.

Chapter 13 - Maintain Positive Wholesome Relationships

*All who obey Allah and the Apostle are in the
company of those on whom is the Grace of Allah –
the Prophets, the sincere lovers of Truth, the
witnesses who testify and the righteous who do
good. Ah! What a beautiful fellowship!*
Holy Qur'an, 4:69

People, like food, can add to the energy in your body, thus
invigorating your energy or lower it – causing you to become toxic
and sick. The reverse is also true – you can enhance or pollute the
energy of others through your presence and interaction with them.
Like any entity in creation, relationships are dual in nature – they
can bring much benefit, or cause much detriment and harm.

As a human being (the crown of creation), your free will gives you the power to transform your intellect and emotions to higher levels and thereby change the quality of the energy you project and/or receive. The increasing ability to successfully do this leads to increased levels of health and wellness and will yield the true peace that your soul is seeking. Ramadan certainly is a time, like no other, when this can occur as relationships are at an unparalleled high and much positive energy, high regard and loving concern are exchanged between fasting believers. Perhaps, this is mainly because restraining the tongue and keeping harmful speech from being expressed, whether in angry tirades or gossiping whispers, is expressly forbidden during this Blessed Month. In fact, engaging in either extreme can result in nullifying your day of fasting which cannot be made up.[23]

Some Muslims, even before the Fast begins, try to find a way to strengthen relationships with others by seeking to learn if they have done anything that was offensive or hurtful during the course of the year leading up to Ramadan. They then, sincerely apologize and ask for forgiveness whether the slight was real or perhaps wrongly perceived by the other person. This strategy provides an opportunity to clear the air and releases any negative energy that believers may have towards one another. Freeing channels of emotional clutter, makes it easier to get closer to Allah and adhere to His Words that govern their lives as they fast, engage in prayer and read the Holy Qur'an.

Allah's Command to put the best construction on matters should call your attention to attribute only the best of intentions to people and to regard even their mistakes and misguided actions in a higher light. When this is done, you may learn that their intentions may not be to do harm but is the result of deep personal hurt or conflict. If so (and you are to assume this), then it becomes easier to embrace them with understanding and to truly want for them what you want for yourself – which first and foremost for the believer, is Allah 's Forgiveness and Mercy.

Timeless wisdom states that, as human beings, we have no power to change others – only to change ourselves. The impact of your working to bring about personal change will be that others will be positioned to respond to you differently. So become the change you are seeking in others. Set the example. Surely this is the gift and the miracle that Allah created in the prophets for us. All of them, from Adam to Muhammad, possessed excellence in character that we can learn and draw life lessons from. Hopefully, by us seeking to emulate these superb men (and women, i.e. the four perfect women), people in our circle of influence will over time learn and draw life lessons from us.

As Muslims, we believe Prophet Muhammad (saw) was the completion in the line of prophets and is the most evolved and comprehensive example for mankind. Therefore, in addition to reading the Holy Qur'an during the month, take time to (re)-read the sirah (life story) of the Prophet which, in rich detail, recounts the beautiful qualities and countenance that makes him the best demonstration of human conduct for all time. After all, it's difficult to pattern your life after someone whose example you know nothing of. And, in striving to emulate him you, too, will become a rich example for others. The following is a partial list of some of his attributes that will be excellent to practice during the special, rewarding time of Ramadan.

- Reliance on Allah, Alone.

- Mindful of Allah's Presence at all times
- Sincerity and truthfulness
- Kindness and compassion
- Gentleness with all creatures
- Cooperation and generosity of spirit
- Bravery and courage
- Excelling in acts of worship
- Not exceeding the limits set by Allah
- Hoping for goodness, even for his enemies

Hopefully you will read, learn of and work to adhere to others.

This month is also a great time to enhance social relations with family, friends and neighbors who are *not* Muslim. It was the way of the Prophet (saw) to show human love, respect and concern for those who were not Muslims. He would make personal visits, especially when ill, share his possessions and give them counsel when they were in need. He never forced or coerced anyone to accept Islam. People were drawn to know more about the mighty influence and force that shaped and developed him as an example and the words of truth that poured from his lips. If you take this approach with others, the results will likely be the same.

In addition to how you relate to others, it is important to know how to healthily relate to all things in creation, animate or inanimate. Knowing how to show love and concern whether it be to an ant, a tree, a lake, your car, home or clothing is essential in sustaining personal health and well-being. Why? Because the more positive energy you exude towards everything in your surroundings, the more positive you will become in your own state of being. You, too, will be contributing to the synergistic flow of positive energy throughout the planet that, through Allah's Plan and Design, is ushering creation into a new awakening and a transformative existence.

Treat everything with respect, love and care. Have a positive mindset that doesn't complain or bring negative emotions into a situation. Do you know that every time you conceive any type emotion, be it joy, fear, anger or excitement, there is a corresponding chemical released within your body that reinforces and embellishes these feelings? If you think positive thoughts endorphins (hormones such as serotonin, dopamine, etc.) will flood your system and make you feel even better. However, if your mind is occupied with negative thoughts then stress chemicals (such as cortisol) will be released, making you feel worse. The mind-body connection is very powerful and proves that, to a great degree, we create our own personal realities. Understanding this, we must take responsibility for our thoughts as well as our actions. Surely Allah (SWT) has said in His Book that on the Day of Judgment every action, thought and feeling will be inquired into and we will have to answer for them.

When Ramadan ends, continue building on the buoyancy of good feelings and enhanced relationships experienced during Ramadan by being committed to put forth your best effort in interactions with others, no matter what! Remember to forgive and overlook as Allah enjoins upon us in the Holy Qur'an. For certainly Allah says in His Book, why do you not forgive others, do you not want Me to forgive you (for your mistakes and sins)?

Reflection:
1. What will you do to enhance relationships in your life this year? Who will you forgive? Who will you seek to connect

with that can enhance your life and that you can enhance theirs?

2. What character traits do you see modeled in Prophet Muhammad (saw) that you need to work on developing more within yourself?

3. What "things" are in your possession that you need to take better care of? (i.e. car, clothes, house, property) How do you commit to do that?

Chapter 14 - Strengthen Your Soul's Connection

Your creation and your resurrection is in no wise but
as an individual soul . . .
The Holy Qur;an 31:28

When looking around at the physical world which appeals to our human eye and intellect, it's easy to become dazzled by its outer manifestations and forget that it's what we *don't* see that is its core reality. Nowhere is this truer than in regards to our personal selves, particularly in relation to how we perceive our health. When we think about our health, usually it's in regard to how we look on our exterior or the physical sensations we feel inside our bodies; this, of course, represents a very limited aspect of our identity. Our true self is our soul – the ethereal essence within us which far outlasts the earthen vessel which carries it throughout this realm of our existence.

Our nafs (soul) is what will be returned to the presence of its Creator, Allah (SWT) upon our physical death. It is what will receive reward or punishment on Yaum al Qiyam, the Day of Standing before Allah in Judgment, which will extend our lives into the infinite realms of eternity either in a state of heavenly bliss or wretched misery. It is the soul that is the prima donna of our existence, the lead performer in the human drama we are playing out in this life and the majority of our time and focus should be devoted to its cultivation and development.

At no other time of the year is there a better opportunity to engage in this spiritual grooming than during Ramadan! The soul is the essence of our human makeup; however most people swept into the intense activity of modern life are oblivious of its ever present reality. The busyness in our outer worlds and the mental activity in our inner worlds usually hinder us from feeling the magnitude of its subtle, but powerful presence. The Fast of Ramadan attunes our sensitivity to reconnect with this oft-neglected part of ourselves. Practicing the rituals of the Fast while seeking Allah's Pleasure as the sole focus of our daily lives, allows our soul to step center stage into its rightful place and have its existence more vibrantly felt.

In preparing for Ramadan, look increasingly for moments when you can be still and experience what it's like to be present with your soul and its connection with your surroundings. Being "present" means that you are fully attuned to life, as it is happening in the moment, so that your thoughts and activities are not a barrier to the aliveness of this connection. It is when sights, sounds, smells and whatever sensory input you receive are speaking "loudly" in your consciousness, making you much more aware of your soul's intrinsic connection with everything around you. You may suddenly notice the piercing sweetness of a bird's song, the rhythmic hum of your refrigerator's motor, the soft insistency of your beating heart, the smell of honeysuckle drifting through an open window or the brilliance of color bursting from a tiny corner of a painting on your wall. Things that were there all along, but you simply were not aware.

It is the connection with your soul that allows you to experience the immediacy of these vibrant energies pulsating all around you. Ideally, you can identify and engage in these quiet "loaded" moments during practice fasts leading up to Ramadan. Many of the exercises and recommendations outlined in this book will enhance your ability to make this connection. When you focus attention on caring for your body and cultivating your mind, your soul is nourished with what is needed to thrive in its ability to receive signs and signals from the world Unseen. Staying well-hydrated with pure water, eating quality, life-enhancing foods, as well as taking in larger quantities of oxygen through deep breathing are vital practices that facilitate the flow of soul energy throughout your being. You will feel more alive in your communication with Allah in your Salat, your du'as, while reading and reflecting on His Words in the Holy Qur'an and throughout the hours of your daily Fast.

Slowing down the busyness of your life, including rapid-fire thoughts, will allow you to become more sensitive to the subtleties of your soul self. To effectively accomplish this, you must minimize environmental and internal noise – loud sounds, TV, internet, intrusive conversations, analytical thoughts, mental chatter (criticism of self and others) – all major deterrents to gaining access to the core reality of your internal existence. Eliminating these superfluous influences, as much as possible, provide an opening through which to connect with the inner you. This inner reality is something to get to intimately know, love, respect, honor and value above anything else in your human makeup.

When you listen, your soul will tell you many things. It embodies the wise intelligence found in every cell of your body. It can tell you what foods to eat, how much of them to eat, when to eat them and how best to prepare them. It can whisper to you when it doesn't feel "right" by creating tightness in your muscles or discomfort in your gut. If you don't pay attention it may "scream" at you by giving you pain or a chronic dis-ease that you experience bodily, mentally and/or spiritually. It has the capacity to let you know what it needs for healing, and what it longs to have for deep satisfaction and *soul* fulfillment. Also, it can prompt you to which people and circumstances to be drawn to and those to shy away from; and it can guide you to the right choices for taking the optimal direction in your life.

Strengthening your body-mind-soul connection is essential so that your soul's energy and intelligence continuously flow into your field of awareness. However, the information you receive from your soul is not always correct. While your nafs (soul) is never misled when following the perfect guidance Allah imparts unto it through His Divine Spirit, it is also open to other energies, emotions and influences. The spiritual heart is considered to be the "seat of the soul" where guidance is communicated from the Divine Ruh (Spirit), however the heart is also host to the vast array of emotions and intense feelings experienced in human life. You must learn the difference between the two – true guidance and emotional feelings; all too often, clear lines of distinction are vague and can be misinterpreted.

Anger, fear, sadness and hurt frequently are deep "heart-felt" emotions that trigger people to act based on the assertion they are justifiably carrying out what is in their soul – therefore rationalizing behaviors that are hurtful to themselves and others. Many violent crimes, obnoxious behaviors, personal and family conflicts and wars are instigated by misguided individuals who erroneously believe their intense feelings are spiritual inspirations communicated from G-d, which give credence to their spiteful words and heinous acts. On the other hand, emotions filled with over-excitement, exuberance and confidence can spark people to say and do things not in their or other's best interests; they, too, believe that these intense passions are directives sanctioned by their Creator.

In Islam, it is taught and understood that the soul, as a distinct entity within the human framework, consists of three states of existence.

The Nafsun Ammara – is the soul state of base desires. Many of these desires arise as a result of living in a flesh body which has various primary instincts that drive its need to survive, i.e. food, security, love, comfort and sex. These instincts in themselves are not bad and are essential for our existence in this material world. Yet, if not tempered with Allah's Commands that establish limits for correct and appropriate human behavior, then mindlessly giving into these desires and "exceeding their limits" will lead to our downfall.

The **Nafsun Lawama** – is the soul state of consciousness and conscientiousness. In this state, the intellect is alive and aware of its responsibility in directing the soul to conform and surrender to the Fitra (natural human pattern) conferred by the decree of Allah (SWT). When the soul resides in this condition, it is questioning, discerning and evaluating its intentions and actions as it relates to the Divine precepts for human living commanded by Allah in the Holy Qur'an and established in the example of His Prophet (saw).

The **Nafsun Mutmainna** – is the soul which comes to be at peace and rest. It exhibits absolute faith and trust in Allah (SWT), has learned through trials and struggles to make the choices that are pleasing to Him and, as a result, it is pleased and deeply satisfied with itself for having completely surrendered. It has become Muslim (not only in nature, but in conscious deeds) – one who has devotedly submitted his/her whole self to the Will of G-d, the object and fulfillment of all of life – in this world and in the next.

Many Islamic books on the topic of the soul identify these conditions as the soul's stages of development, suggesting that we start off on the bottom level and throughout our life gradually work our way to higher states, if we are blessed to do so through our own efforts and Allah's Mercy. I believe this is true to some extent, but that in reality we probably toggle back and forth between these states so that the soul's growth is not linear in movement (suggesting completing one stage of development before moving to the next) but travels in a circular motion between these three states depending on our intentions, understanding and actions in various circumstances. While this may still not be an accurate depiction of soul behavior, one thing is certain and that is the purification and true development of the soul is a lifelong pursuit which we never fully master. However, actively engaging in this quest, much and often, will earn Allah's Pleasure, Mercy and His ultimate Great Reward! Suggested reading material under Resources at the end of this book, contains excellent information on this topic and can be very beneficial in preparing you to seek the deep and profound spiritual benefits of Ramadan.

The only way to understand the distinction of energies coursing through the human heart/soul is by committing to the study and reflection of Allah's Word and Command in the Holy Qur'an and the life of Prophet Muhammad (saw) who best exemplified the application of Qur'anic knowledge in regards to human feeling, thinking and actions. It is the Holy Qur'an, the Final Communication from the Lord of the worlds, that grants guidance needed to discern the true from the false. When looking into the nature of creation, which possesses the duality to lead or mislead the human mind and heart, the Holy Qur'an is the criteria provided so that we can be lead aright.

Sometimes even with regular religious study, you may not readily know or be certain that you are following the best guidance for your particular circumstances. Sometimes, it's difficult to determine the direction in which Allah is guiding you, especially when it's not a matter of choosing right over something that is obviously wrong. Many Muslims, after years of study, devotion and sacrifice have passed this test. What is important is choosing what is best not only for yourself, but for all concerned in a matter – the *khairun*. This is certainly not an easy nor readily attainable task so you must keep moving forward on faith, and trust that Allah is leading you based on the best of your intentions and efforts.

Making Salatul-Istikhara before executing actions on major matters was a very important practice of Prophet Muhammad (saw). When you make this special Salat petitioning your Lord for guidance, make it with complete confidence and with clarity in your intentions and plan of action. Go forward thereafter knowing without question that Allah (SWT) will either open doors for you or deny you if your request will be harmful to you or others.

Know that religious practices alone may not be enough to bring an experiential connection with your soul. There are those who consistently pray, fast and do good deeds, but still feel no internal, intimate bond that brings them closer to their Lord in a way that they long for. This can be due to too strong an attachment to their human form and surroundings, their material possessions, or that they are not mindful and present while performing their religious practices so they are fully conscious of the intent and purpose as to why they are doing them.

If any of this resonates with you in your current spiritual development it may be because you have not pursued enough Scriptural knowledge (of Al-Qur'an) or reflected on how best to apply its knowledge to your everyday life. Or perhaps you are disconnected from your inner life due to distractions and busyness of outer circumstances and internal mindless chatter. Whatever the case, unless you seek to remedy it and proactively make changes to unify your professed beliefs with true and deep Iman (faith and trust in Allah and the excellence and beauty of your natural human Fitr) you will experience inner conflict and schisms in your practice of the Deen. This misalignment will trigger imbalance and distress on many levels. Then, with your body, mind and soul not lined up in support of the growth and evolution of your human development, sickness and dis-ease will manifest – spiritually, mentally, emotionally and/or physically.

What is the distinction between religion & spirituality? Religion is the awareness and belief in Allah as the Creator and Ultimate Authority, and seeking to learn the prescribed practices required to live according to His Command. In a general sense, religion encompasses reading and studying Scripture, seeking useful knowledge, praying as prescribed, fasting as prescribed and giving in charity. It is the foundation and structure for understanding the communication from G-d and His Plan for His human servants.

Spirituality is the cultivation of our hearts, minds and bodies so that they are softened to receive Allah's words, signs, messages, principles, laws and precepts. Through this cultivation we build a bridge between our soul and the loving Presence of our Creator. Spirituality grants us *certain knowledge* (yaqin) in our hearts that allows us to recognize without question that Allah's Promise is true; and through His Attributes we develop an ever deepening understanding of His Divine Reality.

Religion gives us the Divine Communication and the Divine Structure to lead us in the right direction so we have knowledge of the boundaries and parameters in life that will keep us on the Straight Path. We must have religion so we won't stray in our spirituality. However, using our spirituality will enhance our religious practices and give them true meaning.

Spirituality opens our souls to receive and experience joy, satisfaction and fulfillment in connecting and contributing to the oneness in creation. Religious precepts represent ordered growth and development while *spiritual bonding* represents flowing energy that increases our awareness of worlds known only through faith and sensitive connectivity. We can't have one without the other.

Here are some suggestions for enhancing and increasing your religious knowing and your spiritual connectivity before, during and after the Blessed Month.

1. Develop a habit of identifying moments during your day when you can be in a still, quiet space to listen to what's going on within. Cultivate the discipline to remove yourself from internal and external noise. Doing this successfully, for even five or ten minutes a day, will allow you to

gradually develop an increased sensitivity to your soul and will enhance your ability to perceive the information and wisdom it is constantly seeking to communicate to you.

2. Learn to distinguish between the internal voices that you hear. The gentle, firm, positive and affirming voice is more than likely the true whisper of Divine Guidance communicated to you through the Divine Ruh (Spirit) and it is this voice that should be valued and honored as a Sign of the direction Allah wants you to take in regards to your life. When adhering to this voice you feel a sense of calm, assurance and peace. However, if you receive thoughts edged with tones that are harsh, negative, condemning, biased or very limited in scope then know that is the influence of Shaitan or jinn, your own base desires or the erroneous influences of others. When you act on the promptings of these voices you will feel anxiety, tension, conflict and distress.

Remember, Allah says His Signs will appear on the outer horizon and also will come from within. So, seek to know your soul's true voice above all other internal voices. Any other voice is a contending influence which you want to develop the ability to identify and ignore.

3. Commit to reading and reflecting on the Holy Qur'an daily. Even if you only have time to read in very small amounts, reading a section or an ayat a day will allow you to gradually, yet consistently ingest Allah's Words, Signs and

Wisdom for the benefit of *your* soul. You also will be building Qur'anic acumen that will assist you in developing discernment in identifying the authentic voice of Guidance from within. By reading the sirah of the Prophet (his life example) you will also more readily understand how to utilize the Signs in Qur'an for recognizing guidance emerging from within.

When seeking to read the Holy Qur'an for understanding and insight, don't be content to simply recite Arabic words that you have not yet learned the meaning of. You may have to depend on the English translation (or the translation in your native language) for a while, but make firm intentions and a strong effort (within a stated timeframe) to start the process for learning to comprehend the Qur'an in its original text of Arabiyya. The Arabic language is so intensely rich and comprehensive that often there are no equivalent words in English (or words in any other language) that can match its expansiveness, depth, and specificity of meaning. Therefore, when you read Qur'an in any language other than Arabic, you receive only a shadow of the Message that Allah intends for your soul's true elevation and development.

4. Remembrance of Allah is the greatest force in life without doubt. Therefore calling on Him and celebrating Him often in your thoughts, your du'as, your dhikr and your Salat will make you constantly aware and appreciative of your dependency on Him as your Primary Source for guidance and direction. We can be drawn to many powers and influences that manifest in our world other than those that

come from Allah (SWT). (This reflects the state of nafsun ammara.) To truly practice monotheistic worship and live the proclamation that there is no God (i.e. power or influence) but Allah, you must constantly examine all matters from within and without to determine whether they align with the True Reality of G-d's Power and Influence. (This reflects the state of nafsun lawama.) Only then will you truly be in surrender and submission to your Lord. Only then will you have peace and the deep satisfaction within your soul that you have attained the true object of life. (This reflects the state of nafsun mutmainna.)

Reflection:

1. What do you notice when you are quiet and still? What does your soul connect with?

2. What "soul state" are you most often in right now – nafsun awwama, lawanna or mutmaina?

3. What do you need to work on in order for your soul to reach or maintain a level of fulfillment and peace that is pleasing to your Lord and pleased within itself?

Chapter 15 – Keeping It Going Until Next Ramadan

And Allah has subjected to you, as from Him, all that is in the heavens and on earth: behold, in that are Signs indeed for those who reflect.
The Holy Qur'an 45:13

By now, I pray you've had a successful completion of your Ramadan fast and a joyous bountiful Eid! Also by now, insha'Allah, you've developed a clearer sense of the direction your life is to take based on the natural talents, gifts and intellect you believe Allah has placed in you to contribute. Hopefully, too, you learned to incorporate improved dietary habits and personal life choices into a healthier daily regimen as you traveled throughout the Blessed Month experiencing its refining flames of purification and enlightenment.

But, now the real challenge begins! How do you keep the residual benefits and blessings of Ramadan flowing in your life until next Ramadan? Here's a suggested formula for aiding your success and likelihood in being able to do so. Insha'Allah.

Review the material in this manual to make sure you understand the basic concepts and core strategies presented for each topic. Particularly, pay close attention to recommendations for maintaining healthy improvements after Ramadan.

Also, review your personal responses to the questions at the end of each chapter. If you kept a daily journal noting your progress throughout Ramadan, include this information to chart your course over the next weeks and months for sustaining the victories you achieved as well as for strengthening the challenges you continue to face regarding your health and the fulfillment of your life's vision.

Customize the information you've received in this book by using the fundamental principles given and then creating a personal strategy which recognizes and honors that you are bio-individually unique! What works for someone else may not work in the same way for you. So, remember to listen to *your* body and listen to *your* soul. Listen to the inspiration and insights you receive that help them to grow. **Listen** and then obey!

Commit to make focused intentions towards realizing your vision of true body-mind-soul health. Then commit to a plan of action which will gradually move you towards achieving your goal.
Make sure your plan is flexible and adaptable as it may need to shift depending on circumstances and a wellspring of new information

and fresh insights you will receive throughout your journey. Also seek out educational tools which will aid you in pursuing excellence at every turn!

Don't forget to turn your intentions into specific du'as asking Allah for His continuing Guidance and Help for attaining your success. Particularly, before pursuing life-changing options, perform the Istakharaa Salat asking Allah to augment your actions if they are beneficial to you and others; if not, that He will then hinder you from moving forward.

Most importantly, keep up your daily habit of reading Quran. Having accomplished reading a full juz everyday (or most days) during Ramadan, it should now be quite easy to read at least a few ayats each day. You want to keep your mind firm and focused on the ordered structure of living you are commanded to seek that is pleasing to Him.

Remember to make the learning of Qurannic Arabic (for comprehension) a priority in your pursuit of religious knowledge. Reciting the Quran in Arabic may sound beautiful and may provide a deep sense of accomplishment in memorizing and correctly articulating difficult sounds and passages; but if you don't understand what you're saying then you're not benefitting from the profound Wisdom and Guidance Allah's Words contain. Also, regularly pick up the sirah of the Prophet to increase your knowledge and understanding of his life as the "Quran walking". You can't follow or emulate the life of a leader you know little about.

Be determined. Stay the course. Certainly there will be ups, downs and turnarounds as you diligently make efforts to adhere to your soul's path as increasingly it becomes clearer to you. It is easy to become disheartened when things don't turn out the way you plan. However, your job is not to "make things happen" because literally you can't. Allah, Alone, has the Power to construct circumstances and determine their outcome in perfect accord with His Divine Decree. He is the Best of Planners.

Nonetheless, He has given you a wonderful intellect that enables you to reflect, ponder, discern, intend, design, develop and implement. In addition, you have been provided with free will to make choices and decisions among the possibilities that Allah permits to manifest on your journey. Use these gifts wisely. Constantly seek to enhance your mind and intellect. Don't allow your thinking to become boxed in and limited. Continuously explore and open doors to numerous opportunities and ventures which are elevating, not debasing, your excellent human nature.

Allah has given you a magnificently designed body to execute actions to fulfill the yearnings in your soul in accord with His Will and Plan. Your responsibility and task is to take care of and preserve these natural gifts which are on loan to you in this life. Know that on the Day of Standing (Judgment), the Prophet (saw) has reported that your hands, your feet and all of your human faculties will bear witness for or against you as to how well you did your job.

The reality of this future scenario is collaborated by scientific knowledge which has discovered that ingrained in every cell in our body is pulsating intelligence recording every iota of our earthly experience. So, where will your Record of Deeds come from on that Great (and Dreadful) Day – which will be received in your right or your left hand? Perhaps, it is a compilation of your body-mind-soul intelligence being actively recorded every second in your life – right now!

Have faith and belief. It is unavoidable that there will be times when it appears "nothing is happening". It may even seem that your life and your hard work are going in a direction diametrically opposed to what you are seeking. You may have put forth your best efforts and wracked your brains for resolving stagnancy or negative energy that appears to be draining every bit of strength you can muster to keep pressing on. Events and circumstances seem not to make sense – in your soul you are imploring your Lord to show you what you are doing that is wrong!

But it's possible the answer is "nothing." Whenever believers in G-d frame intentions and are dedicated in carrying them out for His Pleasure and Reward, it can be assured that at some point sheitan is going to seek to throw a monkey wrench in the plans. Who or what is sheitan? "He" is a field of negativity that begins first as a whispered suggestion in the mind or soul which attempts to negate belief and faith in the Infinite Strength, Power, Mercy and Wisdom of Allah (SWT). Listening to these false whispers give rise to negative thoughts and actions that at best dilute our efforts and at worst may completely derail them.

The most immobilizing obstacle to achieving success comes in the form of fear. In some circles, very aptly, fear has been deemed an acronym meaning "**F**alse **E**vidence **A**ppearing **R**eal." Certainly, Allah instructs us in His Book that sheitan has no power over us, but what we give him. So, stepping away from snares of negativity whether within or without (i.e. negativity in people and circumstances) and placing absolute trust in Allah (no matter how dark things may look) will allow you to dissolve F.E.A.R. and regain a forward-acting approach to continue moving ahead with your plans.

Allah is our Wakeel, our Trusting Protector at every turn. Many times we will be taken through disturbing events and challenging conditions so we come to know, without any question or fiber of doubt, that there is nothing or no one else to turn to for Help other than Him! And, to realize He is always guiding us to more enlightening and favorable circumstances.

Enroll support where needed. No man (mind) is an island; no one can advance in life without the help of their fellow beings. Thus, on your personal journey to "khalifah success" you will need, at varying times, the support of family, friends, religious leaders, community members, co-workers, business and health professionals and others. When seeking assistance for achieving greater personal growth and development, it is important to align yourself with those who exude a high charge of positive energy and genuinely have the time, focus and commitment to want to help. Particularly, in regard to pursuing life-changing goals, it is wise to form relationships with those whose beliefs, core values and personal quests are similar to and resonate with your own.

If you are experiencing health challenges, hopefully you are among the growing number of people choosing to forgo total reliance on the allopathic model which requires that you turn your body over to medical authorities who often put you on a litany of drugs, subject you to invasive procedures and tests, and many times have you undergo surgeries more dangerous and risky than the condition or dis-ease itself. Maybe already you have turned to alternative options for healing and improving your health that utilize some form of nutritional, homeopathic or naturopathic modalities. Know, however, that organic foods, natural-based supplements and treatments are not "magic-bullets"; they take time to become effective and most times require long term strategies in order that your body-mind-soul health is truly able to benefit.

Therefore, I don't recommend that you go solo in trying to treat your health conditions with the latest vitamin supplement, nutritional tonic, diet craze or exercise trend. Elicit the aid and support of healthcare professionals who can give you correct information related to the individuality of your biological makeup and guide you to the proper portions and proportions needed for your healing. You may have to pay out of pocket for alternative healthcare support since most service providers are not covered by insurance, but you are worth it! If you are willing to invest your money in fixing up your house or repairing your car, then why not be willing to invest in the proper care and maintenance of your own well-being?

Plus, sickness is more expensive than prevention. Invest a few hundred dollars now in a solid alternative healthcare program and you may save thousands, maybe even tens of thousands dollars in monies paid out later on for prescription drugs, laboratory fees, office co-payments, and the like. And, you will be protecting yourself from the curtailment of quality life, income and productivity resulting from chronic dis-ease, pain and/or loss of faculties or limbs.

I suggest that you keep this manual and refer to it often throughout the year as you develop and continue refining your plan and strategies for achieving your goals. Remember that winners in every field of endeavor frequently use coaches to help them get to their next level of personal success. Contact me if you see yourself being in that group. I can help you more powerfully do what you need to do in order to get to where your heart is telling you that you need to be – body, mind and soul! I am a *holistic* health coach, who can assist you in devising and implementing dietary, lifestyle and spiritually based strategies that can help integrate your whole person into an unstoppable life energy destined to achieve your elite G-d given status as khalifah f'il ard. When needed I will work in conjunction with your healthcare providers, *allopathic, homeopathic or naturopathic,* to give you the best support possible in attaining your optimal level of health and well-being!

Remember if you can see a picture of where you want to go and a vision of how you want and need to be, then Allah, the Lord of all the worlds (i.e. Systems of knowledge) (SWT) will bless you with the inspiration and means to carve out a way to get there. Using the principles of healthy holistic living will fortify you to reach higher and higher levels of productivity and accomplishment in every area of your life. Thus, may the glow from the completion of this Ramadan continue to elevate and illuminate every facet of your life throughout the coming year until you reach the threshold of your Ramadan journey next season! Insha'Allah.

Endnotes

[1]Days of Allah - an awakening on earth when God's Authority will reign in the human consciousness and the perception of time as we know it will be dissolved.

[2] Catherine Rampell, "The World is Fat", Economix, Explaining the Science of Everyday Life; 9-23-10; http://economix.blogs.nytimes.com/2010/09/23/the-world-is-fat/

[3]Erik German and Solana Pyne, "Brazilians Pack on the Pounds", Globalpost; 11-25-10; http://www.globalpost.com/dispatch/brazil/101124/obesity-statistics-health

[4]Deepak Chopra, Reinventing the Body, Resurrecting the Soul, (New York: Random House, 2009), 13

[5]J.H. Tilden, M.D., Toxemia Explained, (World Health Classics, 2007), Revised Edition

[6]Heat exhaustion and stroke – *Heat exhaustion* is when people exposed to high temperatures combined with strenuous physical activities and humidity lose body fluids through sweating, thereby causing dehydration and overheating of the body. Person's body temperature may be elevated, but not above 104'F (40'C). *Heat stroke* is a life-threatening medical condition. The body's cooling system, which is controlled by the brain, stops working and the internal body temperature rises to the point at which brain damage or damage to other internal organs may result (temperature may reach 105 F or greater [40.5 C or greater]).

[7] Pam McCaa, "The Oxygen Miracle", http://www.oxygenmiracle.com/main.htm

[8] Imam Salim Mumin, MALI Institute, interview, "The Power of Breath", The Health and Wealth of Natural Community life, 11-12-12; Station IWDM BlogTalk Radio

[9] Malikah Karim, RYT-100, Yoga Instructor, P.U.R.E. Yoga, interview, "The Power of Breath", The Health and Wealth of Natural Community life, 11-12-12; Station IWDM BlogTalk Radio

[10] Aqiylah Collins, CHHC, RM, Qi to Wellness, interview, "The Power of Breath", The Health and Wealth of Natural Community life, 11-12-12; Station IWDM BlogTalk Radio

[11]Organic - the term "organic" refers to the way agricultural products are grown and processed. Specific requirements must be met and maintained in order for products to be labeled as "organic". Farmers are not allowed to use synthetic pesticides, genetically modified seeds or synthetic or toxic fertilizers. Some produce may be organically grown even if it does not have the label of Certified Organic, which is a government regulating body. Google for more information on this very in-depth and sometime confusing label. The main thing is to make sure your food is grown in safe soils without pesticides or harmful fertilizers and that it is not genetically modified.

[12] Marc David, The Slow Down Diet, (Rochester, Vermont: Healing Arts Press, 2005), 78.

[13] Doulliard, John, "It's Mucus-Making Season" http://lifespa.com/its-mucus-making-season/

[14]Halal and tayyib – halal and tayyib are Arabic terms used together throughout the Qur'an. Halal means lawful and tayyib means excellent. Therefore foods and meats we eat should be both. However, much of the food designated as halal may not really be, because it is not also tayyib. Many times halal meat comes from animals that are not raised properly because they have been given unacceptable feed (i.e. pork, chemicals, hormones) and because they were mistreated. http://www.soundvision.com/info/halalhealthy

[15]Aggie Nashid, Raw Foodist, Inn the Raw, interview, "Nurturing & Healing Your Body with Food", The Health and Wealth of Natural Community Life, 11-26-12; Station IWDM BlogTalk Radio

[16] Insulin resistance – is when insulin produced by the body fails to effectively distribute glucose to cells throughout the body. As a result, the glucose (sugar) stays in the bloodstream and wreaks havoc with bodily processes. Often a precursor to diabetes.

[17]Sumayya Allen, Environmentalist, interview, "Nurturing & Healing Your Body with Food", The Health and Wealth of Natural Community Life, 11-26-12; Station IWDM BlogTalk Radio

[18] Haneefah Salim, Certified Personal Trainer, Fitness Life Professional, interview, "How to Get Your Body Grooving & Keep It Moving", The Health and Wealth of Natural Community Life, 2-4-13; Station IWDM BlogTalk Radio

[19] Ibid.

[20] Bertram Brooks, Registered Respiratory Therapist , Technical Director for Southern Sleep Studies, interview, "Wake Up and Get a Good Night's Sleep", The Health and Wealth of Natural Community life, 1-7-13; Station IWDM BlogTalk Radio

[21] Compiled from Dr. Mercola, 29 Secrets to a Good Night's Sleep, http://articles.mercola.com/sites/articles/archive/2010/10/02/secrets-to-a-good-night-sleep.aspx

[23]Quote (pg. 86) http://www.apa.org/helpcenter/job-stress.aspx

[24]Note (pg. 89) The rule for making up days missed during the Fast applies only to those who are physically ill, on an extended journey (*50 miles or more*) or mentally incapacitated – this last one is in the event that the mental challenge is temporary – otherwise they are exempt. Ignoring or neglecting fasting injunctions does not apply to this rule and therefore does not allow for these type infractions to be made up.

Suggested Resources
Books, classes, websites, health and business services for further enlightenment, development and healing

The Holy Qur'an - suggested English translations (3): Yusef Ali; Omar [Noor Foundation International]; Muhammad Asad

Ramadan, Tariq, In the Footsteps of the Prophet, (New York, N.Y., Oxford University Press, 2007)

Farid, Ahmad, Purification of the Soul (compiled from the works of Hanbali, Jawziyyah and Ghazali); (Al-Firdous Ltd., 1992) online e-book available at www.kalamullah.com/Books/PurificationOfTheSoul.pdf

Mogahed, Yasmine, Reclaim Your Heart (San Clemente CA, FB Publishing, 2012)

Muslim American Logic Institute [M.A.L.I.] – online classes teaching Quranic Arabic and grammatical analysis for comprehension of Quran, www.muslimamericanlogic.com

Footsteps to Wellness – holistic health coaching service for adults and children providing individual and group coaching; workshops and classes, www.footstepstowellness.net

Fitness Life Professional – online and on-site personal training and fitness assessments; www.fitnesslifepro.com

P.U.R.E. Yoga – Vinyassa yoga classes; www.pureyogarva.com

Qi to Wellness – Reiki, Birkhram Yoga and health coaching; www.qitowellness.com

Find a naturopathic doctor - www.naturopathic.org

Truly Living Well – urban agriculture, market, training and classes; www.trulylivingwell.com

www.localharvest.org – online locator for farmers' markets, family farms, and other sources of sustainably grown food in your area

www.lumosity.com – online brain games and training for improving cognitive function and creating new neural pathways – loads of fun!

TLC Consulting Services – planning and development services for businesses and non-profit organizations, **www.tlcscdc.com**

The Halal Businesses – a directory & assistance for halal businesses in support of Muslim schools, **www.thehalalbusinesses.com**

The Health and Wealth of Natural Community Life blogtalk radio program – discussing how to create greater levels of health, wealth and well-being for individuals, families and communities; every Monday 8:00 – 9:00 PM. **www.blogtalkradio.com/station-iwdm**

Suhoor Recipes

More recipes available at
<u>www.footstepstowellness.net</u>

Green Energy Smoothie Recipe

1 apple or 1 cup of fresh fruit (do not use melons)

2-3 medium raw carrots

A handful of fresh sprouts (sprouted lentils, adzuki & mung beans are recommended or can use other kind. *You can sprout this yourself—see* **www.foostepstowellness.net** *for sprouting directions*)

1 Tblsp. dulse, or kelp or chlorella (i.e. powdered seaweed—look for at health food grocery, but if you can't find, try using powdered alfalfa, wheat grass or barley)

4-6 leaves of green chard or kale (if very large leaves use 2 or 3)

1 avocado (you may use 1/2 avocado if you like)

Good water (i.e. spring, distilled, alkaline or filtered)

- Place fruit, carrots and sprouts in blender with enough water to blend until smooth
- Then add leafy green vegetables, seaweed and avocado and fill blender with water to cover.
- Blend at top speed until smooth. Add a little water at a time if consistency is too thick.

Makes about 24-32 oz. depending how much water you use. Suggest drinking 8-10 oz. at a time. Try to drink within 3 days. The mixture will not go bad after then, but will not have its full potency.

Note: You can add other fresh green produce—*spinach, dandelion, parsley, cilantro or celery. And you can add herbal seasonings such as ginger, thyme, basil, cayenne or garlic.* (Mustard or collard greens are too strong for this smoothie.) **Pick and choose whatever you like.**

You can also add a little agave or honey for sweetener or organic apple juice. Lemon or lime juice is also delicious blended into the mixture or squeezed into your glass before you drink. Have fun and experiment. Make it different each time!

Healthy Breakfast Frittata

Prep and Cook Time: 20 minutes   **Serves 2**

Ingredients:

1/2 medium <u>onion, minced</u>
4 medium cloves <u>garlic, chopped</u>
1/4 lb ground lamb or turkey
1 + 2 TBS chicken <u>broth</u>
3 cups rinsed and finely <u>chopped kale</u> (stems removed)
5 omega-3 enriched eggs
salt and black pepper to taste

Directions:

1. Mince onion and chop garlic let them sit for 5 minutes to enhance their health-promoting benefits.
2. Preheat broiler on low.
3. Heat 1 TBS broth in a 9-10 inch stainless steel skillet. Sauté onion over medium heat, for about 3 minutes, stirring often.
4. Add garlic, ground lamb or turkey, and cook for another 3 minutes on medium heat, breaking up clumps.
5. Add kale and 2 TBS broth. Reduce heat to low and continue to cook **covered** for about 5 more minutes. Season with salt and pepper, and mix.
6. Beat eggs, season with a pinch of salt and pepper, and pour on top of mixture evenly. Cook on low for another 2 minutes without stirring.
7. Place skillet under broiler in middle of oven, about 7 inches from the heat source so it has time to cook without the top burning. As soon as the eggs are firm, it is done, about 2-3 minutes.

Source: **www.whfoods.com**

Raw Oat Muesli

1 cup rolled oats

1/3 cup walnuts, almonds or unsalted sunflower seeds

1 – 2 apples sliced in small cubes or

1 small banana sliced

1/4 cup raisins or 4-6 dates cut up

1/4 cup dried coconut (optional)

2 cups almond or soy milk

Place all ingredients in a covered bowl and soak overnight.

The next morning, stir and dig in for a creamy textured oat cereal mix bliss.

Chai Spice Pancakes

Serves 2 (makes 4 large pancakes)

The nutty scent of toasting whole wheat flour makes these pancakes really special.

2/3 cup whole-wheat pastry flour
1/4 teaspoon salt
2 teaspoons baking powder
2/3 cup almond milk or soymilk
1/4 teaspoon freshly ground black pepper
1/4 teaspoon ground cloves
1/4 teaspoon ground cardamom
1 teaspoon ground cinnamon
2 teaspoons freshly grated ginger
Nonstick cooking spray (optional)

Mix the flour, salt, baking powder, pepper, cloves, cardamom, cinnamon, and ginger together in a metal bowl. Add the milk to the dry ingredients and mix them until they are well combined. Put this mixture in a measuring cup. Using a nonstick pan (or a pan lightly sprayed with nonstick cooking spray) on medium heat, pour 1/3 cup pancake batter onto the middle of the pan. When the top side bubbles and is mostly firm, flip the pancake over. Keep this on the heat for another 1 to 1½ minutes. Repeat until you've used all the batter.

Source: *21-Day Weight Loss Kickstart* by Neal Barnard, M.D.; recipe by Jason Wyrick of the Vegan Culinary Experience

Tofu Breakfast Scramble

Serves 2

Extra-firm tofu, when crumbled, has a scrambled egg texture and a bit of an egg-like flavor, without the heaviness.

8 ounces firm tofu – (make sure you get organic or non-gmo)
½ onion
½ green or red pepper sliced
1 tsp. curry
1 tsp. cumin
½ tsp. salt
Bragg or tamari soy sauce to taste

Crumble the tofu in a mixing bowl. Heat coconut or sesame oil over medium to high heat. Sauté onion and peppers for 1 – 2 minutes. Add seasonings and stir. Add the tofu and thoroughly mix with seasonings and sautéed vegetables. Cook it for about 3 to 4 minutes. Sprinkle Bragg Amino Acid or tamari soy sauce to taste.

Iftar Recipes

More recipes available at
www.footstepstowellness.net

Carrot Coconut Soup

Ingredients:

1 large onion, chopped
1 TBS + 3 cups chicken or vegetable broth
2 TBS fresh ginger, sliced
4 medium cloves garlic, chopped
1 tsp curry powder
2 cups sliced carrots, about 1/4-inch thick
1 cup sweet potato, cut into about 1/2-inch cubes
5 oz canned coconut milk
salt and pepper to taste

Directions:

1. Chop onion and let it sit for at least five minutes.
2. Heat 1 TBS broth in a medium soup pot. Healthy Sauté onion in broth over medium heat for about 5 minutes, stirring often.
3. Add garlic and ginger and continue to sauté for another minute.
4. Add curry powder and mix well with onions.
5. Add broth, carrots, and sweet potato and simmer on medium high heat until vegetables are tender, about 15 minutes.
6. Add coconut milk.
7. Blend in batches making sure blender is not more than half full. When it's hot, and the blender is too full, it can erupt and burn you. Add salt and pepper to taste.
8. Return to soup pot and reheat.

Source: **www.whfoods.com**

Chicken Cabbage Sauté

Ingredients:

4 cups sautéed or steamed cabbage, sliced thin
1 TBS extra virgin olive oil
1 TBS rice or apple cider vinegar
1 tsp tamari soy sauce or Bragg Amino Acid
1 TBS minced ginger
1 medium clove garlic, pressed
2 TBS chopped cilantro
4 oz cooked chicken breast, shredded or cut into 1" cubes

Directions:

Toss all ingredients together and serve.

Quick Black Bean Chili

Directions:

Ingredients:

1 medium onion, chopped
2 cloves garlic, minced or pressed
2 cups or 1 15 oz can (BPA-free) black beans
1 15 oz can diced tomatoes
1 TBS chili powder
1/2 cup cilantro

1. Chop onions and mince or press garlic and let sit for at least 5 minutes to enhance their health-promoting properties.
2. Place all ingredients—except cilantro—in a pot, **cover**, and let simmer for about 20 minutes.
3. Top with cilantro and serve.

Source: **www.whfoods.com**

Curried Lentils

Ingredients:

1 cup orange lentils, washed
4 cups + 1 TBS vegetable **broth**
1 medium **onion, chopped**
3 medium cloves **garlic, chopped**
2 medium **carrots, diced** into 1/4-inch pieces
2 medium **celery stalks,diced** into 1/4-inch pieces
2 cups finely **chopped kale**
2 tsp curry powder
1 15 oz can diced tomatoes (do not drain)
3 TBS **chopped fresh cilantro**
salt and black pepper to taste

Directions:

1. Rinse lentils in strainer and sort through, removing debris.
2. **Chop** onions and garlic and let sit for 5 minutes to bring out their hidden health benefits.
3. Heat 1 TBS broth in medium soup pot. Healthy Sauté onion in broth over medium heat for 5 minutes stirring frequently, until translucent.
4. Add garlic, carrots, and celery. Continue to sauté for another couple of minutes. Add curry powder and mix to bring out its flavor.
5. Add rinsed and drained lentils, 4 cups broth and tomatoes. Bring to a boil, reduce heat to medium low, and simmer uncovered until lentils and vegetables are tender, about 5 minutes. Add kale and simmer for another 5 minutes. Add cilantro and season with salt and pepper to taste.

Source: **www.whfoods.com**

Bok Choy Stir Fry

Ingredients:

1 bunch bok choy or kale or spinach
2 tablespoons olive oil
2 cloves garlic, diced
½ red or yellow bell pepper, diced
Pinch of sea salt

Directions:

1. Wash bok choy and separate greens from stems, chopping stems into smaller pieces.
2. Heat oil in a skillet and add garlic, sauté for 1 minute.
3. Add bell pepper and cook for 2 minutes.
4. Add stems of bok choy and sea salt and cook until stems become tender.

Add greens and cook until wilted.

You can also add broiled chicken breast or fish fillets for a complete and filling meal.

Tropical Banana Treat

Ingredients:

2 bananas
4 tsp cashew, almond or peanut butter
1/4 cup grated coconut

Optional:
2 TBS dark chocolate chips

Directions:

1. Peel bananas and cut in half crosswise, then lengthwise, trimming the ends.
2. Spread 1 tsp of the nut butter on each flat side.
3. Place the coconut in a saucer and dip the slices into the coconut covering the nut butter completely.
4. If using chocolate, press into the nut butter (optional).

Simple Fruit Compote

Makes 4 1/2-cup servings

2 cups sliced fresh peaches (peeled, if desired)
2 cups hulled fresh strawberries
1/2 cup white grape juice concentrate or apple juice concentrate

Combine all ingredients in a large saucepan. Bring to a simmer and cook for about 5 minutes, or until fruit just becomes soft. Serve warm or cold.

Ramadan Journal Template

Keeping a journal during the Fast gives you an opportunity to capture your inspired thoughts, track your physical health and to review what you've done to work on your personal development each day.   You can download copies of this template to create your own personal Ramadan Journal at **www.footstepstowellness.net.** Or you may want to purchase a special notebook for recording your thoughts and insights.

Ramadan _____ Day/Date_____

Ayat for the day

_____
_____
_____
_____

Goals for the day

_____
_____
_____
_____
_____

Completion of Quran juz: y or n
Completion of 5 daily salat: y or n
Completion of Supererogatory salat: y or n

Food eaten at suhoor

_____
_____
_____

Food eaten at iftar

_____
_____
_____
_____ _____

Water intake ____ oz.   Deep breathing: y or n

Type of
exercise/movement_____

_____

How does my body
feel?_____

_____

_____

_____

Reflections &
insights_____

_____

_____

_____

_____

_____

_____

_____

_____

_____

_____

_____

_____

_____

_____

_____

_____

_____

_____

_____

_____

_____

_____

Ramadan Menu Plan

for the Week of _____

Copies available for download @ wwwlfootstepstowelness.net

Day/Date	Suhoor	Iftar
Sunday		
Monday		
Tuesday		
Wednesday		
Thursday		
Friday		
Saturday		

Ramadan Activity Plan

for the Week of _____

Copies available for download @ wwwlfootstepstowelness.net

Day/Date	Indoor Activities	Outdoor Activities
Sunday		
Monday		
Tuesday		
Wednesday		
Thursday		
Friday		
Saturday		

About the Author

Laila Qadira Yamini is a Certified Holistic Health Coach who lives in Stone Mountain, Ga. with her husband of 18 years, Abdul Hakim Yamini. Through her business Footsteps to Wellness, LLC, she provides nutritional and lifestyle coaching programs, workshops and classes for adults and children. . She is a graduate of the Institute for Integrative Nutrition in NYC and is a student of Qurannic Arabic with the Muslim American Logic Institute [M.A.L.I.]

Website: **www.footstepstowellness.net**

Email:　**footstepstowellness@yahoo.com**